TROUT PONDS AND LAKES
IN THE
UPPER PENINSULA
OF MICHIGAN
AN ANGLER'S GUIDE

TROUT PONDS AND LAKES
IN THE
UPPER PENINSULA
OF MICHIGAN
AN ANGLER'S GUIDE

By Christopher L. Deubler

Siskiwit Press

Published by: Siskiwit Press
2606 School Street
Two Rivers, WI 54241

ISBN: 0-9654303-2-4
LCCN: 99-93585
Copyright 1999 by Siskiwit Press.

DEDICATION

To Ellen and Gemma,
thanks for your dedication
and patience during this project.

ACKNOWLEDGMENTS

First, I would like to extend a special thanks to my wife, Ellen, for the time she has spent typing the manuscript and drawing the maps that accompany this book.

No trout fishing book could be written without the help of fishing partners, which make a project such as this one all worthwhile. Therefore, I would like to thank the following stillwater trout anglers, Robb Deubler, Jeff Parks, and Paul Zagata, for helping gather invaluable information and for listening to my somewhat lengthy and windy discussions on trout biology and management.

Also, it is appropriate at this time to thank A&J Printing for their time, effort, and dedication towards this book and past projects.

CONTENTS

Acknowledgments V
1. Introduction...1
2. Types of Trout Ponds and Lakes 7
3. Trout Species 17
4. Tackle and Equipment 23
5. Selected Fly Patterns and Spin Lures 35
6. Trout Food Sources and Their Associated Stillwater Strategies 41
7. A Selection of Trout Ponds and Lakes 61
8. A Listing of Trout Ponds and Lakes..91
   Addendum: Conservation and Preservation
   Appendix I: DNR District Offices
   Appendix II: National Forests, Parks, and Refuges
   Appendix III: USGS Map Dealers in Michigan

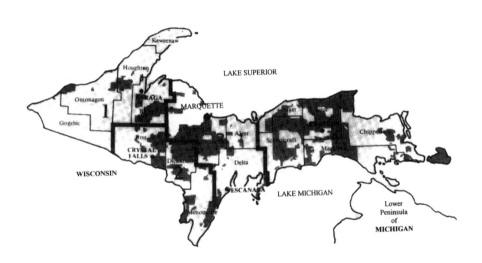

Keweenaw

Houghton

LAKE SUPERIOR

Ontonagon

BARAGA

MARQUETTE

Gogebic

Alger

Iron

Chippewa

CRYSTAL
FALLS

Schoolcraft

Mackinac

Dickinson

Delta

WISCONSIN

ESCANABA

Menominee

LAKE MICHIGAN

Lower
Peninsula
of
MICHIGAN

CHAPTER 1

INTRODUCTION

HISTORIC UPPER PENINSULA

Upon entering the deep, dark forests of the Upper Peninsula of Michigan, early pioneers encountered vast watersheds that must have seemed endless. Nearly impenetrable swamps and bogs mixed with rugged terrain made traveling difficult, if not impossible. Those hardy souls that bushwhacked their way up creeks and rivers to their headwaters found ponds and lakes surrounded by spruce, tamarack, and alder. Here, as if frozen in time, were the hidden jewels of the U.P. left behind by the last glacier several thousand years ago. What an awe inspiring view this must have been for those with the tenacity and stamina to make such a pilgrimage.

As I reflect on this serene image for a moment, I can not help imagining native brook trout leaping out of the still water after dancing midges playing upon the surface. One can only wonder what it would have felt like to be the first trout angler to view such primeval beauty for the first time. While waiting in anticipation for the first strike, this pioneer angler must have had a few thoughts about the size and type of trout that inhabited this northern domain.

Much has changed throughout the U.P. since that eventful day when the first angler cast his line upon the waters of a remote pond. The first and foremost changes occurred when loggers ravaged the land throughout the latter half of the 1800s.

During this relatively short period, the virgin white pine forests that had stood the test of time for centuries were devoured by logging companies that swept across the north country. Left in the wake of this destruction was a raw and barren landscape dotted with massive stumps. Sadly, the era of the great white pine forests had come to an end.

In time, the scarred landscape would heal as various hardwoods along with smaller conifers would spring forth and replace the once majestic forests. Eventually, this new growth would become the lush green forests that provide a paradise for outdoor enthusiasts throughout the U.P. today.

TROUT FISHERY

As loggers opened up new areas, railways and roads began to extend into the heart of the U.P. that was formerly inaccessible except by foot or birchbark canoe. With access now available to many new trout waters, the U.P. soon experienced a dramatic increase in fishing pressure.

Besides resident loggers and miners, wealthy sportsmen would also arrive and sample the tremendous angling opportunities. Photographs from this era testify to this fact as large numbers of sizeable brook trout were caught by these early sportsmen. Over the next century, fishing pressure along with uncontrolled logging practices and large plantings of nonnative fish species would all contribute to a steady decline in the number of native brook trout populations.

As the end of this millennium draws near, pure populations of native brook trout in ponds across the U.P. have been reduced to a mere fraction of their original state. Nevertheless, the adventurous trout angler who is willing to put in the time and effort may still be able to locate ponds that contain pure, remnant populations of native brook trout.

Ponds that harbor pure strains of native trout have never been stocked with trout or been invaded by domestic trout planted in a creek or river farther downstream. Thus, a headwaters' pond containing a pure population of native brook trout will generally be remote and will not be connected to a large trout stream, or a barrier may be present on a pond's outlet creek.

A waterfall or an ancient beaver dam spanning a small creek acts as a barrier by blocking the movement of stocked trout upstream and will prevent the mixing of domestic trout with pure, native stocks above the barrier. Hence, the genetic makeup of a pure population of native trout above a barrier will be preserved if trout are stocked only below the barrier.

Often, an angler may need to hike quite a distance through the brush to reach a pond with a pure population of native trout. However, to be able to catch and release genetically pure brook trout in their original habitat is more than worth an anglers' effort.

If an angler is not inclined to rough it up a creek for a mile or two to a remote pond for pure, native brookies, there are many other ponds and lakes that are easily accessible which hold different species and strains of trout. Many of these spring ponds, manmade ponds, and natural lakes have been generously stocked by the Michigan Department of Natural Resources (DNR) over the years.

Generally, these waters do not hold naturally reproducing populations of wild trout and need to be supplemented on a yearly or every other year basis. For the most part, stocked ponds and lakes make up a large portion of the stillwater trout fishery. Furthermore, stocked ponds and lakes often produce the largest trout due to special regulations and the practice of stocking larger and faster growing strains of trout. In particular, brook trout of the Assinica strain have been known to grow to a hefty size when planted in designated trophy lakes.

Designated ponds and lakes that have been earmarked as trophy brook trout waters are regulated by a 15" size limit and only a single-hook artificial lure or fly may be used. There is a daily bag limit of one trout on these trophy lakes, but it is highly recommended that an angler release all trophy brookies so others can enjoy the fishery, too. Remember, regulations such as these are special and it is important that every angler abide by the laws set forth so that these types of fisheries may continue.

The majority of the stocked ponds and lakes designated as trout waters by Michigan's DNR have a size limit of 10" and a daily bag limit of 5 trout. Some of these designated trout ponds and lakes also prohibit the use of live minnows. This restriction is in place so foreign fish species are not introduced into an all trout fishery. Therefore, to avoid any costly fines every angler should be sure to pick up a copy of Michigan's fishing regulations and familiarize themselves with the laws governing the waters they choose to fish.

MAPS

A map can be a valuable asset when searching for trout ponds and lakes. Since many anglers choose where they fish by county, a good starting point is the Michigan County Map Guide. This guide provides detailed maps of every county in Michigan and will help the angler pinpoint particular areas with concentrations of trout ponds and lakes. Purchasing information for the Michigan County Map Guide can be obtained by writing to the Michigan United Conservation Clubs, Box 30235, Lansing, MI 48909.

If you plan on venturing into a remote area, a much more detailed map is needed. This is where quadrangle maps, also known as topographic maps, can be extremely valuable. To get the big picture of the surrounding landscape an angler should purchase quadrangle maps that have a scale of 1:24,000.

With one of these maps in hand, an angler can plan a route to a pond or lake by using features such as roads, trails, creeks, hills, and swamps. If heading into an unmarked area, it is of utmost importance that an angler have expertise in both compass and map reading. Anglers that are interested in ordering a selection of quadrangle maps should scan the list of USGS map dealers in Appendix III.

RESOURCES

Besides maps, there are various resources available to help the angler plan a trip to the Upper Peninsula of Michigan in search of trout ponds and lakes. The best source of information for planning a trip to a particular area is Michigan's Upper Peninsula Travel Planner. The Travel Planner is alphabetized by town or city and divided into the following sections: lodging, restaurants/dining, and points of interest. There is also a complete listing of all national, state, county, and local parks and campgrounds. There is no doubt that this planner will help the angler take the worry out of planning a trip. Michigan's Upper Peninsula Travel Planner can be obtained free of cost by writing to Michigan's Upper Peninsula Travel and Recreation Association, P.O. Box 400, Iron Mountain, MI 49801 or by phoning 1-800-562-7134.

Another valuable resource available to the trout angler is the DNR fish manager in the area you choose to fish. Fishery personnel at DNR district offices will be able to answer most of your questions relating to trout ponds and lakes. An angler may want to ask questions pertaining to recent trout plantings, naturally reproducing trout populations, special regulations, and access points. For a complete list of DNR district offices anglers should check out Appendix I.

BITING INSECTS

The trout angler that ventures after the wily trout during the warm days of late spring and summer needs to be aware of the multitudes of biting insects that prevail in the wetlands of the Upper Peninsula. Before an angler plans to set foot in the deep woods, it is important to prepare for the onslaught of mosquitoes, black flies, deer flies, and noseeums.

Insect repellent sprays and lotions containing DEET are the forms of protection preferred by most backwoods anglers. In most situations these products will do an adequate job. However, a mesh jacket and headnet soaked in a strong DEET formula is a much more effective weapon for protecting an angler against black fly and noseeum attacks.

*   *   *   *   *   *   *   *   *   *   *

On a final note, wherever you choose to angle for trout take some time to plan your trip to its fullest. The beautiful scenery and outstanding trout fishing which abound throughout the U.P. will be enjoyed much more by the angler who has covered all the bases.

CHAPTER 2

TYPES OF TROUT PONDS AND LAKES

Ranging from the most accessible waters with boat ramps and campgrounds to backwoods waters deep in the interior of the national forestlands, the Upper Peninsula of Michigan offers the angler a diverse selection of trout ponds and lakes. Therefore, the angler's choice is nearly endless.

From a resource standpoint, the stillwater trout fisheries of the U.P. can be classified under the following three categories: lakes, spring ponds, and manmade ponds. Beaver ponds, which are found just about everywhere, will not be discussed in this book, although newly created ponds can provide some fantastic fishing for wild brookies.

The waters within each of the categories mentioned above have unique biological, physical, and chemical features. It is the combination of these features that will determine the productivity of a given piece of water. As you will see, not all trout ponds and lakes have been created equally.

LAKES

Lakes were formed throughout the Upper Peninsula of Michigan by glacial activity that occurred over 10,000 years ago. During the last glacier, large deposits of ice moved across the land and scoured out lakes of all sizes and shapes. As the ice melted and receded, massive amounts of rock and other debris that were carried by the glacier were left behind in these hollowed out depressions.

Three types of natural lakes, drainage, seepage, and spring lakes, were carved out by glacial activity. Originally, only drainage and spring lakes connected to trout creeks or rivers contained native brook trout. Brook trout invaded these inland waters from the ocean via ancient waterways. As the waters receded, brook trout found a home in these icy, springfed ponds and lakes dispersed throughout the Upper Peninsula.

Both drainage and spring lakes have well-defined outlets. However, all drainage lakes have inlets, whereas spring lakes or ponds consist of water received from inflowing springs. Spring ponds which are a unique fishery resource and one of the last strongholds of native brookies in the United States will be discussed in greater detail in the following section.

Seepage lakes, on the other hand, are completely closed systems with no inlets or outlets present. The main water sources for seepage lakes are deep springs and precipitation. Many of these waters were at one time devoid of all fish species. Today, some of the coldest seepage lakes are planted with trout and provide excellent put, grow, and take fisheries.

Depending on the watershed or a particular area in the U.P., the words lake and pond are often used interchangeably to represent a body of water. Maps will occasionally interchange these words, too. Throughout this book, larger bodies of water will be referred to as lakes, while smaller waters will be called ponds. Spring and manmade ponds, which are often labeled as lakes on maps, will be defined in the next two sections to help the angler differentiate between the types of stillwaters that contain trout. Classifying stillwater trout fisheries is quite useful when planning trout management strategies.

Lakes can be classified as being eutrophic or oligotrophic depending on how nutrient rich a particular water is. Eutrophic lakes are extremely rich in dissolved nutrients such as nitrates and phosphates, whereas oligotrophic lakes are low in nutrients.

Due to an abundance of nutrients, both plant and animal life thrive in eutrophic lakes. Areas with large weedbeds will have high concentrations of dissolved oxygen and will attract large numbers of fish. Most stillwaters in the U.P. that fall into the eutrophic category are too warm during the summer to provide suitable habitat for trout. However, nutrient rich spring ponds or lakes that have constant inflows of cold spring water often produce large numbers of trout when adequate spawning areas are present.

Although they are nutrient poor, oligotrophic lakes often provide the right conditions to sustain a trout population. Many oligotrophic lakes that are planted with trout have cold, well-oxygenated water at certain depths. Trout, nevertheless, can not be planted in large numbers due to the lack of available food sources. Minnows, midges, and plankton often provide the necessary food sources to sustain a viable trout fishery, although other food sources such as scuds, crayfish, leeches, caddisflies, and mayflies may be present to a lesser degree.

During the summer, deep lakes will often stratify into three prominent layers. The upper level known as the epilimnion will have the warmest water temperatures. Directly below the epilimnion is a transition zone called the thermocline. This layer is often very narrow and separates the epilimnion from the lower layer called the hypolimnion. The hypolimnion possesses much colder water temperatures than the other two layers. When fed by underwater springs, the hypolimnion will be extremely cold and well- oxygenated.

Deep lakes that stratify during the summer are often referred to as two-story lakes. The upper story will often provide a warmwater fishery, while the lower story may provide a coldwater fishery for trout.

Some lakes and ponds designated as trout waters have been treated with rotenone or other chemicals to remove all warmwater species before trout are introduced. In a few cases, these treatments have failed and warmwater species such as perch, bluegills, and bass are still being caught by anglers. When chemical treatments are successful, trout will not have to compete for available food sources. Thus, trout may be able to grow to much greater lengths with larger quantities of food available throughout the entire lake or pond.

SPRING PONDS

Of the varieties of stillwater trout fisheries available to anglers in the U.P., spring ponds offer the highest quality angling experience. Spring ponds, also known as spring holes, are often found near the headwaters of small trout creeks nestled deep in remote cedar swamps. Many of these ponds still exist in their original settings.

An angler can truly sample a bit of the past while fishing on a wild spring pond. For spring ponds are one of the few fisheries left in the U.P.

where an angler may actually find native brook trout in an unspoiled environment. However, to reach one of these hidden jewels an angler will often be required to put in some extra time and effort.

Spring ponds are associated with terminal or ground moraines left behind by the last glacier. Moraines are highly permeable and ground water flows through the glacial till of the moraines quite easily. Spring ponds will occur wherever kettle holes intercept the ground water table of the moraines. In fact, clusters of these ponds can often be found in areas where these geological features exist.

Certain areas of the U.P. tend to have more spring ponds than others due to the presence of moraines. Stretching on a line from Marquette and Alger Counties to Gogebic and Iron Counties, glacial activity scoured out several hundred spring ponds. These remote ponds are dispersed all along this line with heavier concentrations occurring wherever numerous feeder creeks flow into the headwaters of large trout streams.

The glacier also left behind approximately 2000 spring ponds in the northern half of Wisconsin as it continued moving south. Large populations of pure, native brook trout still exist in Wisconsin due to the fact that there are so many remote spring ponds which are not connected to large trout streams. Unlike large trout streams, the majority of these ponds and the creeks emanating from them have never been stocked with trout. Hydraulic dredging projects coordinated by the Wisconsin DNR have also helped bring dozens of spring ponds back to their original depths and spring inflows, thus strengthening an already thriving resource.

Spring ponds can be defined by four principal characteristics. In combination these characteristics will help the angler differentiate spring ponds from other bodies of water.

The first characteristic common to all spring ponds is that spring seepage or inflows contribute the majority of the water. In essence this characteristic defines spring ponds more than any other.

These nutrient rich inflows are the main reason that spring ponds are one of the most prolific types of stillwater trout fisheries in terms of trout production and biomass. Aquatic plants such as *Chara* and *Anacharis* thrive in these nutrient rich waters. In turn, these plants provide a home for a tremendous number of aquatic invertebrates, which are a constant food source throughout the year for spring pond trout.

Every spring pond has an outlet stream. Outlets can range in size from as small as a few feet to over 20 feet wide. An outlet with a steady flow of water over a gravel bottom may provide a vital link to the trout productivity of a spring pond with limited spawning grounds. Brook trout residing in a spring pond with limited spawning gravel will often use the outlet for building spawning redds. Thus, a wild brook trout population in a spring pond system will continue to exist with this significant link.

Besides being potentially beneficial to a spring pond fishery, an outlet can also have one drawback. An outlet connected to a large trout stream can provide an avenue for stocked trout to enter a spring pond. Unfortunately, the mixing of pure and domestic stocks can cause irreversible damage to the original gene pool.

Another characteristic common to spring ponds is directly related to water moving in and out of a pond. The hydrologic exchange time or flushing rate is the amount of time it takes for the water at any given moment to completely flush out of a pond. In general, most spring ponds have flushing rates of less than 10 days.

Two factors can contribute to a much slower exchange time. The first factor involves the size of a pond or complex of ponds. Due to sheer size and volume, spring ponds with the largest surface areas will usually have the longest exchange times. It stands to reason that the exchange time would be greater if there is more water to be flushed out of a pond.

The second factor involves the damming of an outlet of a pond. Frankly, it does not matter whether a dam is formed by beaver or man. Neither type of dam is very beneficial to a spring pond. A dam built across an outlet will slow down the hydrologic exchange time of a pond considerably. This will cause an increase in the surface water temperature as spring inflows decrease appreciably.

Over time, a slower rate of exchange will produce a heavy buildup of sedimentation, which often results in the covering of vital spawning grounds. Resident trout living in a spring pond that is dammed will not be able to use the outlet stream for spawning purposes either. Consequently, a population of wild trout can be decimated in a matter of a few years if the obstruction is not removed. Besides logging and draining the wetlands surrounding a spring pond, damming a pond at its outlet is the next most destructive force.

The last characteristic defining spring ponds is size. The vast majority of spring ponds in the Upper Peninsula of Michigan have surface areas of less than 10 acres. Spring ponds in this category will often have faster exchange rates than larger ponds. Moreover, a relatively fast exchange rate coupled with sufficient depth has been shown to be positively correlated with high trout productivity in spring ponds.

Spring ponds are a unique trout resource that need to be protected. Those spring ponds that still have pure, remnant populations of native brook trout should receive the highest priority. To preserve these precious stocks certain steps will need to be taken. First, waters designated as native trout ponds should receive extra protection by replacing outdated regulations with more stringent bag and size limits. Some of these ponds could possibly be placed in a catch and release category for even greater protection. Next, beaver activity around outlet areas will need to be controlled so that optimum exchange rates can be maintained. Finally, logging operations that are too close to these wetland environs will need to be monitored to protect the areas encompassing spring ponds. If these measures can be put in place, the remaining pure stocks of stillwater brook trout in the U.P. will finally be ensured a safe haven.

MANMADE PONDS

As the title of this section would suggest, these ponds were created by man with the help of heavy duty machinery. Many of these ponds were constructed for the sole purpose of providing additional put, grow, and take trout fisheries. Small campgrounds and easy access sights for canoes and small boats were also developed to complement a few of these trout ponds. Thus, outdoor enthusiasts that are interested in combining camping, canoeing, and trout fishing without roughing it too much will find these ponds to be quite enjoyable.

There are primarily two types of manmade trout ponds: ponds formed by dams and borrow pit ponds. Those ponds that were formed by building earth walls across small creeks are the most common. The majority of these creeks are trout waters with very limited natural reproduction or none at all. Therefore, these dams do not pose a threat to the trout fishery present in most of these creeks.

Trout ponds that were formed unintentionally by pits being dug for other purposes are found to a lesser extreme than trout ponds that were formed by dams. Old, abandoned borrow pits that filled in with water provide suitable habitat for trout if cold, oxygenated water is present. Although they are only a small portion of the stillwater trout fishery in the U.P., borrow pit trout ponds can provide some good fishing.

Manmade trout ponds that were formed by placing a dam across a small creek primarily receive water through precipitation and the creek itself feeding in at the top end of the pond, although some ponds receive substantial spring inflows. During drought years, some manmade ponds will suffer because of extremely low water levels and high water temperatures that are lethal to trout. However, trout ponds that were formed by building dams at the springheads of small creeks will usually maintain viable fisheries throughout the entire fishing season due to the presence of proper oxygen levels and water temperatures.

There are primarily two ways that water will exit trout ponds that have been formed by manmade dams. In the first type, water will exit via a culvert. Water exiting a pond will flow down the culvert that is often placed at the end of the dam. The diverted water will then be routed out the backside of the dam as the creek continues on its course. These manmade ponds may become stagnant during the summer due to a reduction in the rate of exchange.

The second type of dam has a simple cement spillway placed strategically along the earth wall. Ordinarily, this type of dam does not have any mechanical device to control the flow of water and the outflow is generally reduced to a mere trickle during low water conditions. Thus, the water level in most manmade trout ponds can not be regulated due to the types of dams in use.

Unfortunately, manmade ponds formed by these types of dams may be drawn down severely during a drought and will not provide suitable habitat for trout. Trout residing in ponds of this type will head upstream looking for sustainable water temperatures during low water conditions. Hence, an angler may want to venture up the inflowing creek in search of trout when these conditions exist.

Ponds that are formed by dams will always have a major problem with siltation. Because of the inflowing water slowing down when it reaches a pond, sediments will be deposited instead of dispersing farther downstream in a watershed. Indeed, some ponds receive heavy loads of sediment from inflowing creeks, particularly during spring runoff.

Heavy weed growth is positively correlated with rich, mucky substrates often found in ponds formed by dams. As decomposition takes place in late fall, weedbeds add to the sedimentation process. Over time, the bottom of a pond will grow thick with muck, while the depth of a pond may decrease dramatically.

Weedbeds can also be beneficial to a pond. Large masses of aquatic invertebrates thrive in these dense weedbeds and are the principal food source for trout residing in ponds. Chubs, shiners, and dace are also commonly found in ponds that have large weedbeds. Minnows such as these will provide a steady forage base for trout greater than 10 inches in length.

The size and type of trout planted will vary from pond to pond depending on available living space, food sources, and water temperatures throughout the year. Ponds formed near springheads have colder supplies of water than other manmade ponds and are primarily planted with brookies. Luce County has several ponds of this variety to choose from that are quite fertile and productive. Other ponds that were formed farther downstream on small creeks will often become too warm for brook trout in summer and will receive plantings of brown trout. If larger food sources such as minnows are plentiful, brown trout will grow to sizeable dimensions in these ponds.

Manmade trout ponds that were formed by borrow pits filling up with water are closed systems much like many of the stocked trout lakes across the Upper Peninsula. Borrow pit ponds that have bountiful supplies of spring inflows will maintain proper water temperatures and oxygen levels to support trout throughout the year. Due to the absence of spawning grounds, borrow pit ponds need to be stocked on a yearly basis. However, since they are somewhat nutrient deficient, borrow pit ponds can not sustain too many trout at one time.

Due to the fact that they were dug in areas with heavy loads of sand, rock, and gravel, some borrow pit trout ponds may have very little weed growth. Many of the aquatic invertebrates that are found in eutrophic waters may not be present in borrow pit ponds. Zooplankton, midges, and minnows form a suitable but somewhat narrow food chain that trout will feed on at various stages of life.

Except in a few cases, the majority of stocked ponds and lakes in the U.P. are planted with sublegal trout. This also holds true for borrow pit trout ponds. Waters in this category such as the Roxbury Ponds in Chippewa County usually receive a few hundred brook trout in the 3- to 7-inch range, thus providing a put, grow, and take fishery where anglers can catch and release smaller trout before the legal size limit has been reached.

In their own way manmade trout ponds provide a special type of stillwater trout fishery. Since many of these waters can be reached without too much difficulty, manmade ponds can be accessed by anglers with limited mobility or by anglers that are just looking for a relaxing day of fishing. In either case, manmade trout ponds can provide anglers with an interesting diversion from other types of trout water.

CHAPTER 3

TROUT SPECIES

For generations anglers throughout the U.P. have had a love affair with trout fishing. As spring rolls around each year, anglers turn their thoughts toward opening day. Melting snows and rising temperatures summon anglers to prepare their gear for the new trout season. Prior to the big day restless anglers will search through an endless number of maps and stocking reports before choosing a trout water to fish, while others will choose to haunt their perennial favorites.

When opening day finally does arrive, trout anglers will be out at the crack of dawn in search of the first trout of the season. Trout anglers in the U.P. will often have to buck snowdrifts or plow through quagmires to reach their destinations. Once there, anglers must then brave icy, cold temperatures in pursuit of the wily trout. Nevertheless, diehard trout anglers will go forth no matter what conditions exist.

Over time, trout fishing fanatics will often develop certain preferences. Some anglers may fish for only a single species of trout, whereas other anglers may fish only a particular type of water.

Anglers that prefer fishing trout ponds and lakes will find a variety of trout species to choose from. By far the most common trout species found in ponds and lakes throughout the U.P. is the brook trout. Both wild and domestic populations can be found in these waters.

The acrobatic rainbow trout is the next most popular trout species to be found in ponds and lakes. Because of their spectacular leaping abilities, rainbows have become a treasured import. Rainbow trout have done quite well when stocked in two-story lakes where they can take advantage of the coldwater column.

Brown trout are planted in lakes and ponds to a much lesser degree than either the brook or rainbow trout. Manmade ponds that become too warm for brookies during the summer are often planted with browns. Because of the tremendous number of food sources available, brown trout can bulk up very quickly in these ponds. Browns are also stocked in a few select lakes where they can obtain even greater dimensions.

Larger stillwater fisheries that have extremely deep water are often planted with splake and/or lake trout. These species require extremely cold water and must be angled for in very deep water during the summer.

Of the five varieties of trout present in ponds and lakes in the U.P., only brook, brown and rainbow trout will be discussed. Areas that will be covered include classification, origin, description, spawning, food sources, and human influences. Hopefully, the following overviews will give the angler a greater understanding of each trout species.

BROOK TROUT

Brook trout are native to the entire U.P. and have always been a favorite among trout anglers due to its exquisite coloring and delightful flavor. Although it carries the trout name, the brook trout is actually a charr. In fact, the scientific name for brook trout, *Salvelinis fontinalis*, means "charr living in springs." Since brook trout are never found very far from spring inflows, this derivation is somewhat fitting.

Coloration will vary among different populations of brook trout because of environmental and seasonal influences. However, certain characteristics are common to most brook trout.

Brook trout will have greenish-olive to nearly black backs with light wormlike markings known as vermiculations, which truly distinguish the brook trout from other trout species. Light spots interspersed with red spots surrounded by bluish halos are also common. The belly of the brook trout may vary in color from white to bright orange or red, while the lower fins are usually orange and edged in black and white.

The brook trout spawns in fall, which is a common trait among members of the genus *Salvelinus*. During spawning time, brook trout will seek areas with gravel or coarse sand over upwelling springs. Due to their ability to spawn over upwelling springs in ponds and lakes, brook trout are highly successful at reproducing. Survival of brook trout eggs is much higher in ponds and lakes than in streams, because sediments are less likely to smother the eggs. Thus, remote spring ponds or lakes with large spawning areas will often become overpopulated with stunted brookies.

The brook trout is an opportunistic feeder and will very seldom pass up an easy meal. Upon examination, aquatic invertebrates such as midges, scuds, caddisflies, water beetles, and water boatmen are most commonly found in the stomachs of brook trout residing in ponds and lakes. Minnows and leeches are also fed on by large brookies but to a lesser degree.

Because of intense logging, beaver activity, and indiscriminate plantings of domestic trout, many pure, native populations of brook trout have been lost forever. Most of the remaining wild or native brook trout populations occur in remote creeks and spring ponds.

Although they are stocked quite liberally in ponds and lakes throughout the U.P., domestic brook trout will never quite replace the original native stocks. Remote lakes and ponds that are stocked with brookies can, however, provide quality trout fisheries. In some instances, ponds and lakes that are too remote for hatchery trucks are stocked in the winter by transporting trout by helicopter. Holes are drilled through the ice in advance, then brook trout are poured into the chosen lake. The most remote lakes are not frequented by very many anglers during the season and provide the highest quality fishing experiences for stocked trout.

Trophy brook trout waters are another type of fishery developed by the state to provide quality fishing. Those ponds and lakes that are designated as trophy waters are often planted with the Assinica strain or a mixed strain. The Assinica strain is a native of Canada and is known for its longevity and ability to grow to much greater proportions than other brook trout strains. When planted in limited quantities, it is not uncommon for brookies of this strain to reach 4 or 5 pounds.

BROWN TROUT

The brown trout is not native to North America and was originally brought over to this country from Germany in the 1880s. In fact, the first major planting of brown trout occurred in the year 1884 in the Pere Marquette River. Since this inaugural planting, browns have been distributed widely throughout Michigan. Many blue ribbon trout streams in the Lower Peninsula have established naturally reproducing populations of brown trout.

The brown trout is a true trout with a very ancient history. The scientific name for the brown trout, *Salmo trutta*, has its roots in Old English and Latin and in essence means the original trout. Writings by Aelianus around the year AD 200 spoke of "a fish with speckled skins" living in a Macedonian river. Presumably, the speckled skinned fish that Aelianus wrote about was the brown trout. If so, this could possibly be the first words ever written about any trout species.

The brown trout has since been glorified by many authors over the years. Izaak Walton wrote of the brown trout quite eloquently in his well known book, *The Compleat Angler*. During this century, Theodore Gordon and Vincent Marinaro wrote extensively about the habits of brown trout after years of observation.

Various color schemes are found among the different strains of brown trout. However, most browns will have olive to dark brown backs shading to light yellow on the sides. The sides are also sprinkled with black and red spots which are encircled with light halos. The belly will range in color from white to lemon yellow, while the lower fins are usually light yellow with black and white trimming.

Brown trout living in deep, clear lakes, however, may be silvery in color much like the rainbow trout. An angler having trouble distinguishing the two species should remember that the tail of the brown trout has very few spots, whereas the tail of the rainbow trout is heavily spotted.

The brown trout is a fall spawner much like the brook trout. In general, spawning activity will take place in late October or November. The female brown trout will usually cut a redd at the tail end of a pool where water washes through gravel substrates. Male brown trout will be attracted by this behavior with the most aggressive males pairing up with spawning females. Dominant males will protect the redd sight from smaller males by nipping at them with their hooked jaws.

The food sources that brown trout will prey on in lakes and ponds will vary depending on the stage of life. Early in life, browns will feed primarily on small aquatic invertebrates. As they grow a bit larger, brown trout will consume a wide variety of aquatic insects and crustaceans. After reaching a length of 12 inches or greater, browns may exclusively become minnow feeders.

Even though it is not stocked very heavily in ponds and lakes, the brown trout does offer the angler a challenge. Older browns that become nocturnal feeders and somewhat secretive can often attain large proportions if ample food supplies are available. Anglers in search of these lunkers will generally have to plan nighttime angling strategies.

RAINBOW TROUT

The rainbow trout is a Pacific Coast native and was originally introduced into Michigan waters in the 1870s. The first shipment of rainbows arrived from a California hatchery. The rainbow quickly found a home in many streams throughout Michigan. Eventually, migratory populations of rainbow trout took hold in the Great Lakes and have become a spring favorite among trout anglers. Although its scientific name, *Oncorhynchus mykiss*, was just assigned within recent years after great debate, the rainbow itself has remained unchanged.

Rainbows will vary in color depending on whether they are found in a stream or lake. In general, wild rainbow trout dwelling in streams will have a beautiful mix of colors. Their backs will range in color from olive green to steely gray with silvery sides. Wild rainbows will also have a profusion of black spots with an iridescent red stripe running along the side. In contrast, rainbows planted in lakes are often dull or much lighter in color than streambred rainbows. Spots will not be as distinct on planted rainbows either.

Most rainbow strains will spawn in spring, although certain migratory strains are fall spawners. During the spawning season, rainbows will pair up at the tail end of larger pools or runs. The mating behavior of the rainbow is similar to the brown trout with the female cutting the redd and the male playing the role of the aggressive defender.

Rainbows planted in inland lakes usually do not have the proper habitat to reproduce. Therefore, the state selects lakes that maintain proper water temperatures and oxygen levels for rainbow trout to survive and then stocks them accordingly. Rainbows have found a niche in the coldwater column of two-story lakes and can provide excitement for the trout angler with their acrobatic leaps.

In the early stages of life, rainbows will feed heavily on plankton and midges in the open water zone. As they mature, larger aquatic invertebrates and minnows become vital food sources for rainbows. Rainbows that survive several seasons of fishing pressure can put on extra fat and attain very hefty weights.

The rainbow trout is a valued resource among trout anglers that prefer lake fishing. Rainbows can provide the angler with an exciting alternative to other trout species as they dance and leap across the surface. Because they are easy to manage and grow quite well in hatcheries, rainbows have also become a favorite among hatchery personnel throughout the United States.

CHAPTER 4

TACKLE AND EQUIPMENT

Collecting tackle and equipment is one of the most cherished pastimes shared among fellow members of the angling world. For some anglers, it is an annual ritual to page through a large number of catalogs in search of the newest angling paraphernalia. As spring fever runs high, the urge to look at new tackle and equipment grows even stronger.

As with any type of angling, different variables come into play when choosing the appropriate tackle and equipment. The type of tackle and equipment required for fishing trout ponds and lakes will generally vary depending on the size and depth of the water, remoteness of the water, clarity of the water, and type of shoreline, although an angler's preferences will also need to be weighed.

The size and depth of a pond or lake will often determine which type of watercraft and method of angling should be used. The smallest trout ponds and lakes are ideal for floating a small boat, canoe, or float tube, whereas larger boats equipped with motors may be the preferred choice for bigger bodies of water. In deep lakes, spin fishing with heavy lures will usually produce better results than fly fishing. In contrast, shallow spring ponds that have enormous midge hatches are highly desirable waters for the fly angler.

An angler hiking into a remote pond or lake will have to place a limit on the amount of tackle and equipment to be transported. One rod and reel combination along with a fishing vest and a pair of waders may be the only gear that an angler chooses to carry to a remote pond or lake. Without the use of a watercraft, however, an angler will usually be confined to the water closest to shore.

The clarity of the water in a pond or lake will determine the length and diameter of the leader and tippet the fly angler should choose. In the clearest ponds and lakes, trout can be quite skittish. Therefore, an angler will need to cast a long, fine leader to prevent the offering from being seen as a fraud. When fishing on tannic stained ponds, leaders can be shortened in length and increased in diameter without the fear of putting every trout down for the day.

The type of shoreline surrounding a pond or lake will often dictate whether an angler should wade or use a boat. Boggy shorelines and mucky bottoms, which are common to many spring ponds, will generally prevent an angler from wading, while sand, rock, and gravel bottoms found along the shorelines of oligotrophic lakes offer ideal wading conditions for the angler.

There is such a wide array of products on the market today that can make it quite difficult for the angler to select the proper tackle and equipment. In the pages to follow, fly fishing tackle, spin fishing tackle, watercrafts and accessories, and miscellaneous tackle and equipment will be addressed in relation to trout pond and lake fishing. It is hoped that this chapter will help the trout angler gain a better understanding as to the type of tackle and equipment that is necessary to be successful at pond and lake fishing.

FLY FISHING TACKLE

Fly anglers are definitely in the minority when it comes to trout fishing on ponds and lakes in the U.P., although there are plenty of opportunities that await those which are interested in casting a fly upon these stillwaters. Before setting forth, however, a fly angler should have a working knowledge of the type of fly tackle that is needed for pond and lake fishing.

When choosing the appropriate fly rod, an angler should keep in mind the size and openness of the water intended to fish. Intimate, little trout ponds that are surrounded by stands of cedar and tamarack will not allow the fly angler to make very lengthy casts nor will they be needed. Fly rods that can make delicate casts with long, fine leaders are definitely in order when presenting a small midge or scud pattern. Preferably, fly anglers should choose rods that are 7 to 8 feet long which are designed to handle 3-

or 4-weight lines. There are a wide variety of rod manufacturers that make very fine, light rods which can handle the most delicate presentations.

Fly anglers that wish to try their hand at fly fishing for trout on large lakes will need longer fly rods matched to heavier lines. Due to the possibility that an angler may face stronger winds on a larger body of water, a fly rod between 8 to 9 feet long matching a 6- to 8-weight line will be necessary. The exceptions on these larger lakes are the coves and bays that can provide protection from strong winds. When fishing in these protected areas, an angler may be able to get away with using a 4- or 5-weight rod.

The majority of the trout that anglers will hook into on trout ponds will be small enough to be handled on a light, single action fly reel. A lightweight rod and reel combination will provide the fly angler with many pleasurable hours of fly fishing without developing a sore arm or shoulder. If perchance a 3- to 4-pound trout is hooked, an angler should be able to follow the trout around the pond without becoming completely spooled. Deadheads and underwater snags, however, may be of greater concern to the angler when trying to play such a large trout.

An angler fly fishing with a sinking line on a large, deep lake may wish to use a larger reel with a stronger drag. The reel should also be equipped with an ample amount of backing in case a large trout is hooked. Large rainbows and browns, which are common to many of the larger trout lakes, can strip quite a bit of line off a reel in a hurry. Therefore, extra backing will come in handy if an angler hooks into one of these leviathans.

Most of the smaller trout ponds are somewhat shallow, especially spring ponds. When fishing on these waters, a fly angler should stick with a double taper floating fly line. Both surface and subsurface presentations can usually be handled with a floating line. For the most part, a weighted fly can be sunk deep enough to present it to trout that are feeding at various levels including right on the bottom. Furthermore, the tip of a floating line can be used as an indicator when fishing nymphs deep on a long leader.

On large, deep lakes, an angler should switch to a wet tip or full sinking line depending on the depth at which the fly will be presented. If the depth of the presentation is not too extreme, a wet tip will provide greater line control and easier pickup than a full sinking line. Full sinking lines come in a variety of sink rates that cover every subsurface angling situation an angler may encounter. Some of the full uniform sinking lines developed in recent years have all but eliminated the problem of line sag in the belly section. Thus, a straighter line and better depth control can be achieved during the entire retrieve with a uniform sinking line. An angler will also be able to detect strikes more frequently with much greater line control.

When presenting a fly on small trout ponds, an angler will need a long, fine leader tapered to 6X or 7X. Some anglers prefer to tie knotted leaders, which may turn over better than knotless leaders. No matter what type you prefer, your leader should be approximately 12 feet in length when fly fishing on small, clear spring ponds. In fact, on clear days, anglers may want to lengthen their leaders even further before presenting their offering. Conversely, on dark, tannic stained ponds, an angler can cut back a couple of feet on the length of the leader without spooking every trout within casting distance.

Leaders should be shortened in length and increased in strength when fishing a deep line. A short, stout leader will provide the angler with greater line control extending all the way to the fly. Direct contact with the fly during the entire retrieve is important or most strikes will go undetected.

Fly fishing for stillwater trout is often challenging but also quite rewarding. Anglers that learn to employ the proper fly tackle will be on their way to becoming proficient stillwater fly fishers. In the following chapters, anglers will discover which imitations and strategies are best suited to trout pond and lake fishing. With these tools, an angler will be able to make educated decisions when trout fishing on stillwaters across the Upper Peninsula.

SPIN FISHING TACKLE

Spin fishing, which is an import from England, hit the angling scene in a big way across the U.P. in the 1950s. With the advent of spin fishing, a whole new world of angling was opened up to trout fishers. Casts that were nearly impossible with bait casting and fly fishing outfits were made easy by the flick of a wrist with spin fishing equipment. Spin fishing even made it possible for a beginning angler to learn how to cast within a matter of hours.

After World War II, the United States economy was thriving and more people began to seek recreational opportunities throughout the state including spin fishing for trout. Right on the heels of this recreational explosion came the bridging of the Upper Peninsula and the Lower Peninsula in 1957. With easier access now available to the U.P. from down state and a large number of anglers converting to the newest method of angling, the trout waters of the U.P. came under assault like never before. Unfortunately, bag and size limits would remain the same, which created the need for large plantings of trout on heavily fished waters.

Since the 1950s, spin fishing tackle has improved with leaps and bounds. Probably the greatest improvements have come in the form of ultralight spinning gear. These lightweight spinning outfits have added an exciting dimension to trout fishing over the years.

Most anglers that spend the majority of their time on the water spin fishing for trout prefer ultralight rods that are 4 to 6 feet in length. The newest of these graphite rods are extremely sensitive, and even the smallest trout will impart action to these rods. Ultralight rods are also perfect for casting small lures into tight spots.

In general, anglers that seek trout in large, deep lakes will employ medium action rods. These rods have the backbone it takes to fight the largest of trout but yet sensitive enough to provide enjoyment when tussling with a 10- to 12-inch trout. Also, larger spoons and spinners often used to reach trout in deep water can be cast with ease by a spin angler using a medium action rod.

An ultralight reel matched with a 4- to 6-foot graphite rod will provide an angler with the perfect combination for angling on small trout ponds. When casting from a brushy shoreline, an ultralight outfit will allow the angler to make long, smooth casts. Where it is not practical or possible to haul a watercraft to a remote pond or lake fringed with cedar and tamarack, the ultralight enthusiast definitely has an advantage over fly and bait casters.

On larger trout lakes, a spin fisher should use a medium weight reel with a stronger drag than that of an ultralight reel in case a trout of 4-pounds or better is hooked. Larger reels also have line capacities that can handle several long runs by an oversized trout.

Depending on the clarity and size of the water, an angler will have to choose a line accordingly. On small, clear ponds, an angler will catch more trout with 2-pound line. Delicate casts with very small lures are the norm on these ponds. Even the slightest splash can send wild brookies swimming for cover. Dark stained ponds or large lakes will not require such a stealthful approach, although the angler may have to fish with a light line on calm, sunny days. An angler should, however, be able to use 4-pound line on the majority of the trout ponds and lakes in the Upper Peninsula without a problem.

Spin fishing has come a long way since its introduction to the U.P. in the 1950s. Although it is the youngest of all angling methods, spin fishing is by far the most popular form of sport fishing today. Many anglers in fact that grew up fishing by other means before spinning tackle was available have since become converts to this way of angling. With its easiness to learn and advantage over other forms of angling on brushy waters, it is no wonder that spin fishing has become the favorite among the majority of trout anglers.

WATERCRAFTS AND ACCESSORIES

Today, stillwater anglers have a wide array of watercrafts to select from. Rowboats and canoes, which are old-time favorites among U.P. trout anglers, have two worthy rivals today, float tubes and one-person pontoon boats. These latter two have opened up new avenues to anglers that prefer fishing remote waters. Each type of watercraft, however, has its advantages and disadvantages, and stillwater anglers will need to weigh these carefully before choosing the watercraft that best fits their angling needs.

With stillwater trout fishing becoming quite popular in recent years, the outdoor sports industry has also created some innovative accessories to complement these watercrafts. Many of these accessories were created to ease the angler's burden, and, in general, will make the angler's time on the water much more pleasurable.

One-person pontoon boats, which are the newest breed of watercrafts, offer the trout angler an exciting alternative to other lightweight crafts. Both inflatable and noninflatable pontoon boats are available to stillwater anglers. Pontoon boats are not only light and portable but comfortable to sit in for long periods of time. Entering and exiting a pontoon boat is relatively easy as these boats are very stable. Most pontoon boats can also be navigated by oar or fin power giving the angler another valuable advantage.

There are a few drawbacks to using a one-person pontoon boat. The most obvious disadvantage is the preparation time needed to inflate the pontoons and assemble the craft. The newest double action pumps, however, can fill the air bladders very quickly, thus reducing the preparation time considerably. Also, pontoon boats are not the best choice on windy days because navigability will be somewhat limited. On blustery days, an angler should find a quiet cove or wait for the winds to subside before venturing forth. Depending on the distance traveled to a pond or lake, the largest pontoon boats may be quite a burden on an angler. Therefore, a trout angler who prefers angling on remote ponds and lakes may want to opt for the smallest of pontoon boats.

Pontoon boats will vary in price depending on the model and options that are chosen. The size and material used to construct the boat will determine whether the angler spends a few hundred or a thousand dollars. Accessories such as rod tube holders, stripping baskets, cargo decks, carrying cases, seat pads, oar locks, double action pumps, and specialized anchors can all add to the cost of the purchase. Therefore, it is of utmost importance that an angler shop around and check out all the different options before buying a pontoon boat.

Probably the most innovative watercraft ever developed for remote stillwater angling has been the float tube. These lightweight tubes are easy to pack and carry in to out of the way ponds and lakes. Over the years, float tubes have definitely been improved upon in the areas of comfort and stability. Very few float tubes are designed today without safety in mind, and most now have tough nylon shells that protect the air bladders from being punctured.

Float tubes do have some disadvantages. First, as with an inflatable pontoon boat, an angler will need to spend some time inflating a float tube. Again, there are double action pumps that can do the job in a short amount of time and get the angler on the water much quicker. Second, float tube anglers are at a major disadvantage on shallow spring ponds. These ponds generally have very mucky bottoms that can make it impossible for float tubers to even enter the water without being sucked up by muck. Third, hypothermia is a real danger to anglers using float tubes in cold water. An angler should, therefore, limit the amount of time spent in the water early and late in the season or select another type of watercraft during the coldest part of the season. Finally, windy days make float tubing quite difficult and somewhat dangerous on large lakes. On the windiest of days, it may be in the angler's best interest to float tube on a smaller body of water or wait until the winds subside.

Different accessories are available to the angler that can make float tubing much more enjoyable. Anglers can buy float tubes with various built-in accessories such as storage pockets, rod holders, backpack straps, D-rings, and adjustable seats. Anglers will, however, need to buy a pair of fins, a double action pump, and a small anchor to complete their float tube itinerary. A stripping basket can also come in handy for storing line when retrieving medium to long range casts.

Canoes are an excellent choice for pond and small lake fishing. Many anglers, in fact, are still quite partial to canoes. Visions of a lone angler in a canoe gliding across the surface of a placid trout pond are deeply ingrained in the souls of outdoor enthusiasts across the north country.

With so many strong, lightweight materials available, companies have been able to develop canoes that are light and durable. These lightweight canoes can be hauled to remote ponds and lakes by two anglers without too much stress and strain.

Canoes do, however, have a few disadvantages. The smallest canoes lack space for two anglers, and it can become very uncomfortable for the angler in the front of the canoe to sit for a long period of time. Therefore, in a small canoe it is best for one angler to cast and the other to paddle for a while to prevent lines from being tangled. Then positions can be changed to allow one angler more leg room and the other a chance to fish.

When heading to a remote pond or lake, larger canoes present a problem for anglers. Here an angler will have to decide between a long, tiresome journey with a bulky canoe or an easier hike in with waders. Sometimes the latter is a much more practical and sane approach.

Old, wood rowboats litter the shores of many north country ponds and lakes. These sunken vessels remind anglers of a different place in time. A time that was slower paced with fewer people and when watercrafts were made entirely of natural products. These heavy boats were a labor of love for their makers and provided a means by which anglers could fish a pond or lake in its entirety.

Most rowboats on the water today are made of aluminum, although some old-timers hold on to the past with their wood boats. Generally, the majority of boat owners prefer aluminum boats, because these lighter crafts are easier to transport and move through the water faster. However, aluminum boats do lack the natural look of wood that meshes very nicely with the surroundings of ponds and lakes in the Upper Peninsula.

On larger trout lakes, anglers may equip their boats with motors if allowed by law. Obviously, anglers can get around much quicker on a big piece of water with the use of a motor and can cover more territory in a shorter period of time.

Rowboats are not practical for a great number of remote ponds and lakes in the U.P. because of their size and weight. Anglers that own only a rowboat may want to invest in a different type of watercraft if they wish to angle on a remote pond or lake. Otherwise, they may have to be content with wading and fishing along the shoreline.

Anglers employing canoes or boats will need very few accessories. Paddles, oars, or a motor will provide the means of navigation depending on the watercraft to be used. Anchors will come in handy on windy days and will keep the boat positioned in an area that is producing. Boat cushions are also a necessity and can make sitting for hours much more enjoyable. Lastly, life vests are not only an accessory but must be brought along when fishing from any type of watercraft. Every angler should remember that safety takes precedence over any type of activity on the water.

MISCELLANEOUS TACKLE AND EQUIPMENT

Besides the tackle and equipment mentioned in the categories above, there are other items that may be just as important to the stillwater trout angler. Before departing on a trip, an angler will have to decide which of the miscellaneous items in this section will be needed.

Although the majority of stillwater anglers prefer to use some form of watercraft, there are some anglers that find wading or walking along the shoreline of a pond or lake to their liking. A wading angler will generally need two types of waders to handle the various weather conditions found throughout the trout fishing season in the Upper Peninsula.

In general, an angler will have a choice between the following types of waders: neoprene, breathable, and nylon. Neoprene is a favorite among anglers in cold weather. These waders not only keep an angler warm during cold weather but are also very light. Neoprenes generally cost more than nylon waders and less than breathable waders. The major drawback with neoprene waders is that they do not breath. Thus, an angler can become overheated wearing a pair during the hottest part of the summer.

When fishing in warm weather, an angler should choose between breathable or nylon waders. Breathable waders no doubt offer the angler the most comfort in warm weather, but the cost may prohibit some anglers from buying a pair. Nylon waders are an excellent, inexpensive alternative to breathable waders for warm weather. When fishing in brush country, nylon waders are also much more durable. During cold weather, however, neither breathable nor nylon waders will keep an angler warm for extended periods of time.

A fishing vest is definitely a necessity when trout fishing on ponds and lakes. Not only are most vests quite light, but many accessories can be stored in the pockets of a fishing vest. Vests come in all sizes and styles, and anglers will need to select one according to preference and the type of fishing to be done. Depending on these two factors, items to be carried in an angler's vest may include flies, leaders, tippets, lures, extra line, hooks, a clippers, a hemostat, fly floatant, splitshot, a flashlight, a knife, a tape measure, and an extra reel.

Polarized sunglasses are also a necessity on stillwater. These sunglasses are not only useful for spotting trout in clear ponds and lakes but can be used to help focus on the tip of a floating fly line when fishing subsurface flies. Furthermore, polarized sunglasses can reduce the amount of dangerous UV light that reaches the angler's eyes and can help cut through the glare on the water's surface.

With such a tremendous number of biting insects present throughout the U.P., insect repellent may not always be enough to protect the angler. Therefore, when fishing during the warmer months of the season, a mesh bug jacket soaked in a DEET formula can often save the day. For even greater protection, an angler may want to bring along a headnet. With the combination of a bug jacket and a headnet, the only exposed area will be an angler's hands, which can be covered with insect repellent. These accessories may be the difference between a short, hellish trip that resembles Dante's Inferno or a long, pleasant day in trout heaven.

A landing net may also come in handy when fishing a pond or lake where large trout exist. On a trip to a remote pond or lake, however, an angler will have to decide whether a landing net will be a necessity or a hindrance.

When traveling into remote country, it is always best to play it safe by letting someone know where you are going. Also, it is extremely important that an angler bring along items that are necessary for survival in case one becomes stranded for a day or two. First and foremost, an angler should carry in an ample supply of water. Please do not rely on drinking water out of a pond or lake in the backcountry. Beavers frequent these waters and are often associated with a bacteria called Giardia, which can cause extremely painful intestinal problems. An angler should also remember to pack food for the outing. A trail mix high in carbohydrates and protein is an excellent choice and is easy to pack. Matches should also be packed in case an angler needs to build a fire to stay warm throughout a cold night. Lastly, a raincoat is a necessity as bitter cold rains can quickly chill an angler to the point of hypothermia.

Through trial and error, an angler will discover the tackle and equipment that is needed for a given fishing outing. As an angler gains more knowledge about stillwater trout fishing, these decisions will become second nature. However, until you feel comfortable with your selections, always play it safe by taking too much instead of too little.

CHAPTER 5

SELECTED FLY PATTERNS AND SPIN LURES

Although tackle and equipment may present the largest financial burden to the angler, it is what is on the terminal end of the line that most often determines success or failure on the water. Without the proper artificial attached to the leader or line, all the expensive equipment an angler may own could prove to be quite worthless.

Choosing the proper artificial lure or fly can be quite challenging and at times frustrating when trout refuse to strike your offerings. However, matching proper lures or flies with food sources available to trout at any given moment on a pond or lake is one of the most interesting aspects of trout fishing. It is this challenge that sets trout fishing apart from many other outdoor pursuits.

FLY PATTERNS

Fly anglers are quite fortunate that a large number of fly patterns have been developed over the years which cover a wide variety of food sources present in stillwaters. The following patterns cover the majority of food sources a fly angler will need to imitate on trout ponds and lakes in the U.P. and should also help the angler limit the number of stillwater flies that will need to be carried in his/her vest. When presented at the proper place and time along with the appropriate strategies mentioned in the next chapter, the following fly patterns have proven to be very effective on trout ponds and lakes throughout the Midwest.

NYMPHS

Chironimid Pupa

Hook: Sizes 12-20
Thread: Black
Tail: White floss
Body: Black floss
Rib: Silver wire
Thorax: Peacock herl
Breathing filaments: White floss

Olive Scud

Hook: Sizes 10-16
Thread: Olive
Weight: 10 turns fine lead wire
Tail: Olive hackle fibers
Shellback: Clear plastic
Body: Olive rabbit fur
Rib: Olive thread
Legs: Olive hackle
Antennae: Wood duck flank fibers

Golded-Ribbed Hare's Ear

Hook: Sizes 8-16
Thread: Brown
Weight: 5 wraps of light wire
Tail: Hare's ear
Body: Brown hare's ear
Rib: Fine gold wire
Wingcase: Turkey tail fibers
Thorax: Brown hare's ear

Cased Caddis

Hook: Sizes 8-16
Thread: Brown
Case: 4 soft feathers, plamered and clipped
Wingcase: Turkey tail fibers
Neck: White chenille
Legs: Brown hackle fibers

Sparkle Pupa

Hook: Sizes 10-14
Thread: Brown
Weight: 6 turns lead wire
Body: Brown antron
Hackle: Brown
Head: Brown hare's ear

Water Boatman

Hook: Sizes 10-16
Thread: Tan
Weight: 6 turns lead wire
Shellback: Natural turkey quill
Body: Tan chenille
Legs: Two pheasant tail fibers, one for each side

Prince Nymph

Hook: Sizes 10-16
Thread: Black
Tail: 2 black goose biots
Rib: Silver tinsel
Body: Peacock herl
Hackle: Brown hen
Wing: White goose biots, one on each side

DRY FLIES

Griffith's Gnat

Hook: Sizes 16-24
Thread: Black
Body: Peacock herl
Hackle: Grizzly hackle, palmered

Elk Hair Caddis

Hook: Sizes 10-16
Thread: Tan
Rib: Gold wire
Body: Tan fur
Hackle: Brown hackle, palmered
Wing: Tan elk hair

STREAMERS

Woolly Bugger

Hook: Sizes 6-12
Thread: Black or brown
Weight: 10 turns lead wire (optional)
Tail: Black or brown marabou
Body: Black or brown chenille
Hackle: Black or brown, palmered

Blacknose Dace

Hook: Sizes 8-12
Thread: Black
Butt: Red
Body: Silver mylar
Topping: Natural, black, and white bucktail

Muddler Minnow

Hook: Sizes 6-12
Thread: Brown
Tail: Turkey
Body: Gold mylar
Topping: Squirrel tail with turkey
Collar: Spun deer hair
Head: Spun deer hair, shaped

SPIN LURES

Artificial lures that have been designed for the spin angler generally imitate forage fish. In fact, many of these lures simulate the movements of a crippled or feeble swimming minnow. When presented properly, these lures can produce excellent results on trout ponds and lakes throughout the Upper Peninsula. Strategies for presenting minnow and other spin lures will be described in the next chapter.

Other lure designs that imitate food sources such as leeches and nymphs can also be important to the spin angler. Various lures have even been created in recent years to help the spin angler cash in on certain insect hatches. Thus, spin anglers have a greater variety of lures to choose from than ever before. The lures that follow are only but a small selection of the artificial lures available to stillwater spin anglers in search of trout. However, this selection should cover a wide spectrum of choices for those anglers that elect to fish on waters which require artificial lures only.

Mepps Aglia Spinner

Size: #00, 0, 1, or 2
Color: Silver, gold, or copper

Mepps XD Spinner

Size: #1 or 2
Color: Silver or gold

Rooster Tail Spinner

Size: 1/16 oz.
Color: Silver or gold

Panther Martin Spinner

Size: 1/16 oz.
Color: Black

Daredevil Spoon

Size: 1/32 or 1/16 oz.
Color: Red and white

Rapala

Size: 1/8 oz.
Color: Silver, gold, or chartruese

Timber Doodle

Size: #00 or 0
Color: Black

Thunder Bugs

Size: #00 or 0
Color: Black, brown, gold, or silver

Jigs

Size: 1/64, 1/32, or 1/16 oz.
Color: Black or white

CHAPTER 6

TROUT FOOD SOURCES AND THEIR ASSOCIATED STILLWATER STRATEGIES

The diversity and density of trout food sources within a pond or lake is generally determined by several factors. Those factors that have the greatest influence upon the production of these food sources are weed growth, bottom substrates, chemical composition of the water, and type of shoreline.

Nutrient rich waters, which are associated with large weedbeds and mucky bottom substrates, often produce the greatest number of food sources. A pond or lake with a highly irregular shoreline in relation to its total surface area is also positively correlated with large densities of aquatic food forms. Because of the abundance of food sources within these nutrient rich ponds and lakes, trout will grow quite rapidly.

In contrast, waters that have low nutrient levels generally lack weed growth and the food sources associated with them. These nutrient deficient waters usually have somewhat rounded shorelines with bottom substrates composed of sand, gravel, and rock. Because of the shortage of available food sources, trout will tend to grow very slowly in these ponds and lakes.

An angler does not have to be an aquatic biologist or entomologist to be successful at catching trout in stillwaters. However, when an angler has a working knowledge of the food sources present in a chosen pond or lake, much of the guesswork will be removed. Knowing the food sources present in a particular water will help the angler concentrate on the imitations and strategies that will be most effective. In the long run this means more action and less frustration for the angler.

In this chapter, the angler will discover the food sources that represent a large portion of the stillwater trout's diet. The strategies associated with these primary food sources will also be presented to help stillwater anglers improve their skills on the water.

MIDGES

Midges are divided into six families and are members of the order Diptera, which includes all two-winged insects. The most significant stillwater midge family are the Chironimidae, which are often referred to by anglers as chironimids. Although chironimids are generally consumed most often by stillwater trout, other midge families or species can also be important as food sources.

To put things in perspective, the angler should be aware that several thousand species of midges are known to exist. Thus, it is nearly impossible to make any clear generalizations about the midge species that might be available to any given trout population without a thorough examination.

At first glance, a midge appears to look somewhat like the blood thirsty mosquito, which is a close relative and of the same order as the midge. However, on closer inspection, the angler will notice that the midge lacks the all too familiar stinging mouth part of the female mosquito.

Coloration varies among the numerous aquatic species of midges with the most common colors being black, olive, gray, red, and brown. Midges also vary greatly in size with the largest being about an inch in length and the smallest not much bigger than a speck.

The life cycle of the midge can be broken down into four stages: egg, larva, pupa, and adult. Midges begin their active lives as larvae and are generally found in bottom substrates such as muck, sand, and detritus, although some species cling to algae and submerged weeds. Midges emerge from their burrows or homes once they have reached the pupal stage. At this point, many adult characteristics are also visible. It is during the emergence phase that midges are highly susceptible to trout predation and knowledgeable fly anglers are well aware of this.

During emergence, the weak swimming pupa rises quite helplessly to the surface. Once a pupa reaches the surface, it will rest for a period in full view of feeding trout before hatching. This resting period is often determined by the surface conditions of a pond or lake.

If the surface is calm such as on a warm, humid evening, hatching may be prolonged and pupae may have to wiggle about in the surface film for an hour or more. Under these conditions, pupae may become trapped in the surface film. Feeding trout will have easy pickings when this occurs. On windy days, the surface water will be broken and midges will be able to hatch out very quickly. Thus, midges have a much better chance of escaping the jaws of feeding trout when windy conditions exist.

Once hatched, the adult midge does not normally spend much time on the surface before flying away. However, on calm, humid evenings midges may need more time to dry their wings before attempting to take flight and can often be seen skating across the surface. The observant angler may want to imitate skating adults when a large number of midges are exhibiting this behavior.

FLY FISHING STRATEGIES

Fly fishers that master the strategies for presenting midge imitations will definitely have an advantage over other anglers on trout ponds and lakes. This is because midges are available throughout the entire fishing season and make up the number one food source for stillwater trout.

The type of strategy a fly fisher chooses to use will be dependent on where trout are feeding on midges. Sometimes this takes a very observant eye. This is especially true on the surface where it may appear that trout are feeding on adults when in fact they may actually be feeding on pupae in the surface film. Often, an angler may have to try different strategies before finding the one that is most effective.

Taking a closer look at the life cycle of the midge the fly fisher will discover that the midge is most vulnerable to trout predation during the pupal stage. During its ascent to the surface, the feeble swimming pupa becomes an easy target for feeding trout. Generally, trout prefer to feed on midge pupae close to the surface or near the bottom.

When trout are feeding on or near the surface but are refusing dry imitations, try fishing a Chironimid Pupa in the surface film or suspended just below the surface. The angler should present the fly with a 12- to 16-foot leader tapered to 6X or 7X, which will give the fly a much more lifelike appearance. By greasing the leader up to the last few inches, the fly will suspend below the surface. On calm evenings, the angler can entice trout into striking the fly by giving it an occasional twitch. When making a presentation in the surface film, a small amount of fly floatant should be applied to the fly. Trout can often be coaxed into striking a fly presented this way when they are focused on midges in the hatching stage or when vast numbers of stillborns are present. Again, the angler should give the fly a twitch occasionally if a dead drift is not producing.

There will be many times when the surface will be devoid of feeding trout. This is generally the case when hatches are not occurring or are sporadic. When these situations arise, it is best to fish a Chironimid Pupa on a deep line close to the bottom. By switching to a beadhead pupa, the angler can reach the bottom much faster. Depending on the depth of the water, the angler will have to choose between a floating, wet-tip, or full sinking line. The fly angler should also consider cutting back to a 9-foot leader so that better line control can be maintained during the entire retrieve.

When fishing a midge pattern on a deep line, use a countdown method to find the appropriate level at which trout are feeding. Once the fly is ready to be retrieved, the angler should employ a slow strip and pause technique. The angler can effectively imitate the weak swimming pupa by drawing line in very slowly a foot at a time and then pausing a few seconds to let the fly sink for a while.

Trout will usually strike the fly near the bottom or close to the surface during the retrieve. However, trout can strike the fly very quickly during a pause, so the angler needs to be constantly attentive to any movement of the line.

Trout that are keyed in on adult midges can often be tempted to strike a dry imitation using a couple of tactics. The first strategy involves casting to a particular trout that is sipping midges quite regularly. Using a long, wispy leader, the angler should try to place a Griffith's Gnat very gently upon the surface as close to the trout as possible. This generally elicits an immediate strike from a trout that is gorging itself on adult midges.

Another technique that is useful for presenting an adult imitation is to skate a Griffith's Gnat across the surface to imitate the V-line an adult midge makes when trying to take flight. This strategy works best on very calm days. Trout will often leap entirely out of the water after an imitation presented this way and will sometimes hook themselves on the way down.

FORAGE FISH

Trout that grow to immense size generally do so by feeding on other fish. Once they reach 12 inches or greater, trout will often consume forage fish depending on the food sources available.

Forage fish are quite common in trout ponds and lakes throughout the Upper Peninsula. Many species may in fact have been spread accidentally throughout these waters by anglers using them as bait. On several designated trout ponds and lakes in the U.P., forage fish can no longer be used as bait nor can they be found in the possession of an angler. This is a sound practice and prevents foreign fish species from being introduced into trout waters that have been reclaimed by the state. Thus, on trout ponds and lakes where they are not allowed, anglers will need to imitate forage fish with artificial flies or lures.

Anglers will find a variety of forage fish to imitate in trout ponds and lakes in the Upper Peninsula. The most common forage fish present in these waters can be categorized as minnows, sculpins, and sticklebacks.

These varieties of forage fish display different movements and habitat preferences. Minnows such as chubs, shiners, and dace swim at a slow pace and can often be seen milling around or pausing for short intervals unless they are disturbed. Minnows generally swim in schools and can often be found in shallow water. They can also withstand warmer water temperatures than sculpins and sticklebacks. Sculpins and sticklebacks make short, darting movements while often resting on or near the bottom for extended periods. Sticklebacks are generally found in or around weedbeds, while sculpins prefer bottom materials such as rocks and rubble. Both species do quite well in coldwater ponds and lakes.

FLY FISHING STRATEGIES

Three types of fly fishing strategies will be discussed in this chapter for presenting streamers (fish imitations) in trout ponds and lakes. The strategies to follow will give the fly angler a general overview for presenting streamers near shore, in deep water, and on the surface.

When trout are feeding on forage fish near shore, the angler should present a streamer on a fine leader. Trout feeding on forage fish in shallow water are extremely spooky. Thus, the presentation should be made very quietly.

Using a Blacknose Dace, the angler should cast towards shore, preferably near weedbeds, rocks, or logs. The fly should be allowed to sink a few seconds and then retrieved in short, slow strips while pausing briefly between each strip.

The angler should remember that chubs, shiners, and dace, which often frequent shallow water, move quite slowly unless they are disturbed. Therefore, in shallow water, try to refrain from making sharp movements with the fly that might spook trout which may be nearby.

In deep water, a 5- or 6-weight rod in the 8- to 9-foot range will be needed. The angler will also want to employ a uniform sinking line and a short, stout leader. A weighted streamer or a single splitshot placed right in front of the fly will help get it down to the bottom faster. A Muddler Minnow is an excellent choice for probing deep water.

Again, when fishing a deep line, the countdown method should be used to reach the bottom. After finding the bottom, the angler should retrieve the line a foot at a time and then allow the fly to settle to the bottom before continuing. It is important that the angler keep the fly near the bottom for an extended period so it can be shown to as many trout as possible. Finally, at the end of the retrieve lift the rod up slowly while still imparting movement to the fly all the way to the surface.

Trout can often be seen cruising near the surface in ponds and lakes in search of food. When encountering a school of minnows, trout will generally attack from below. For the most part, the slowest and weakest of minnows will be culled out of the school. Trout need to be energy efficient when feeding and will not chase a single minnow for a long time.

When trout are chasing a school of minnows near the surface, the angler should present the fly by twitching it a few times and then pausing for a couple of seconds. This action will simulate the movements of a weak or crippled minnow. The streamer chosen should be quite light so that it does not sink too far below the surface. Trout will at times strike a lightweight streamer with considerable force near the surface. Thus, a strong leader is definitely a necessity.

SPIN FISHING STRATEGIES

Since the introduction of spin fishing, anglers and fishing manufacturers throughout the United States have developed many ingenious spinning lures. With such a wide variety of lures available on the market, spin fishers should have no trouble finding the appropriate imitation to use for any given situation.

Over the years, lures that imitate minnows have definitely taken a front seat among designers. In fact, many of the best ideas for developing minnow lures have come from those closest to the sport, the trout fisher.

Along with a variety of minnow imitations, the spin angler should also have a selection of strategies to try. Strategies will no doubt vary according to what part of a pond or lake the angler chooses to fish. Whether the angler selects to cast to deep water, near shore, or on the surface, a proven approach is very important.

When working the shoreline, the spin angler should make soft casts with 2-pound line to areas with submerged weedbeds, timber, and rocks. Lures should be scaled down when making presentations along the shoreline, because trout can be quite spooky in shallow water.

After making a cast towards shore, allow the lure to sink a couple of seconds before starting the retrieve. The retrieve should be slow to moderate when imitating chubs, shiners, and dace that frequent the shallows in ponds and lakes. Try to work the lure around underwater obstructions that often harbor some of the largest trout residing near shore. During the early season when trout are lethargic, be sure to slow down your retrieve.

Deep water is probably the most difficult area in a pond or lake to consistently find and catch trout. However, with the latest electronic gadgets available for locating fish, half the game of fishing has been removed. Even if a fish locator is employed, the angler will still have to find a way to entice trout into hitting a lure.

From a stationary position in a watercraft, the angler will want to cover as much territory as possible in deep water. By using the countdown method and making casts one after another in the shape of a fan, the angler can cover one depth at a time quite thoroughly.

After sufficiently covering one depth, the angler should move to the next level. By varying the speed of the retrieve and lure selection, the secrets of the deep should hopefully be uncovered. The angler will be able to cover a large area in the least amount of time when moving about the water from place to place using the fan casting method.

Casting minnow lures to trout near the surface requires a different approach and is generally most productive when trout are chasing minnows. Anglers should always be on the lookout for minnows that are jumping out of the water or making sharp, quick movements near the surface. This is often a warning signal that minnows are under attack by trout on the prowl.

Anglers that are aware of this behavior should try to imitate the quick movements of a fleeing minnow by using a floating imitation and imparting short twitches to the rod tip. Trout that are chasing minnows near the surface will often be enticed into taking a lure that simulates the movements of a fleeing minnow. The angler may wish to vary the speed of the retrieve until a trout finally strikes. If no strikes are forthcoming after covering the area with several casts, the angler should consider moving on to greener pastures.

SCUDS

Among the crustaceans indigenous to ponds and lakes throughout the U.P., scuds are the most important food source for trout. Scuds are members of the order Amphipoda and are often referred to as freshwater shrimp because of their shrimp-like appearance. They will generally range in size from one-third to one inch in length depending on the species. Many different color variations exist among scud populations with olive, tan, gray, and brown being the most common.

Scuds are strong swimmers and quite often swim on their backs. When darting about in open water, the body of the scud will be straight and fully extended. This is very important for the fly angler to remember when designing and imitating the agile swimming scud.

For the most part, scuds shy away from light and definitely prefer moving about during nighttime hours or on overcast days. During the day, scuds often hide in weeds such as *Chara*, *Anacharis*, and watercress. Sand, gravel, leaves, moss, and detritus also offer a home for scuds. By picking up a handful of leaves, weeds, or detritus, an angler can get a good idea of the number of scuds present in a particular pond or lake.

Gammarus and *Hyallela* are the two most common species of scuds found in trout ponds and lakes throughout the Upper Peninsula. Of the two species, *Gammarus* requires the coldest water temperatures and has the least tolerance for pollution. Because they are a larger species than *Hyallela*, *Gammarus* may also be more important as a food source for trout. However, no matter what species is present, large scud populations are usually associated with healthy trout.

FLY FISHING STRATEGIES

In ponds and lakes where they are relatively common, scuds can be imitated at any time during the fishing season. It is best to present scud imitations at dawn or dusk when they are active, although gloomy, rainy days can also be productive.

When presenting scuds close to shore, the angler will need to make a quiet approach. A 12- to 16-foot leader tapered to 6X or 7X along with an Olive Scud or Gold Ribbed Hare's Ear Nymph will work just fine in this situation.

Preferably, the angler should first concentrate on submerged logs and weedbeds. The fly should be placed as close to cover as possible. Often, a trout that is lying nearby will strike the fly immediately upon entering the water.

Once the cast is laid out, the retrieve should be started right away to prevent the fly from becoming snagged on a log or weed. To best imitate a scud, use a hand-twist retrieve mixed with a slow, steady pull of the line. A steady movement of the fly will imitate the free swimming scud very nicely.

Deep water is always a challenge when presenting flies to trout. However, by using a uniform sinking line and the countdown method, the angler can search different levels for feeding trout with some consistency. Once a level is chosen, the fly should be retrieved by slowly drawing line in with an occasional twitch between each draw. At the end of the retrieve, the angler should lift the rod slowly and work the fly all the way to the surface. In clear water, the angler will be able to view trout coming after the fly as it makes its upward swing towards the surface.

CADDISFLIES

Caddisflies are one of the better known aquatic insects among trout anglers. This prolific, moth-like insect can often be seen in large numbers fluttering above shoreline vegetation. When at rest, the wings of a caddisfly are folded back on its body giving them an unmistakable tent-like appearance. The wings of a caddisfly also have a hairy look to them when observed at close range. In fact, caddisflies belong to the order Trichoptera, which when translated means "hairy wings".

Several hundred species of caddisflies are known to exist throughout North America. Caddisfly species range in size from two inches down to one-eight inch in length. Adult caddisflies will also vary greatly in color with brown, olive, tan, and gray being the most common.

Of the species present in ponds and lakes throughout the U.P., case building caddis are by far the most common. It is the case builders that beginning anglers first discover while moving about the shallow areas in ponds and lakes. Case builders are also highly visible to trout, which readily consume them case and all.

Anglers should have a basic knowledge of the larval, pupal, and adult stages of the case builders to better understand them from an angling standpoint. By understanding the different stages of life, anglers should be able to employ the proper imitations and strategies when needed.

In the larval stage, cases are formed by adhering sand, stones, and sticks together with a sticky substance exuded from their salivary glands. As they grow during this stage, larvae often become too large for their cases. When this occurs, they discard the old case and build a new one. This process may be repeated several times.

The larvae of many caddisfly species make their home among the various aquatic plants found in shallow water. Most of these species survive and flourish in ponds and lakes that maintain stable water levels. In contrast, caddisflies tend to do poorly in ponds and lakes that have fluctuating water levels because of their preference for shallow, weedy areas and lack of mobility.

Before emergence takes place, larvae migrate to very shallow water. During this period, larvae seal themselves inside their cases. Transformation from the larval to the pupal stage takes place during their encapsulation. Adult characteristics also become visible at this time and emergence will take place within a couple of weeks.

Caddisflies generally emerge during evening hours or after dark. Some species swim straight up to the surface, while others swim laterally towards shore during emergence. Upon breaking through the surface film, adult caddisflies may behave in two ways. Some species will motor across the surface to shore, whereas other species will dry their wings and flutter about for a while before taking flight. Both types of behavior can cause feeding frenzies when caddisflies are present in large numbers.

Upon leaving the water, caddisflies will seek shoreline vegetation or other nearby objects for refuge. They will often lie in these shaded areas until mating takes place. This period may last up to a month.

Depending on the species, females will either deposit their eggs over the surface of the water or dive below the surface to make their deposit on bottom materials. Adult caddisflies become extremely vulnerable during this stage of life. Fly anglers using the proper imitations and strategies can have some exciting fishing when trout are feeding on egg laying females.

Spent caddisflies will be present upon the surface of a pond or lake the morning following a night of egg laying activity. A large number of spent caddisflies will provide an early morning entree to trout and may ignite a feeding frenzy at daybreak.

FLY FISHING STRATEGIES

Caddisflies can be imitated by the fly angler at every stage of their lives. While on the water, however, an angler will have to determine which stage of life the majority of the trout are feeding on. By carefully observing any hatching activity or migrations of caddis larvae toward shore, an angler should be able to make some decisions as to the appropriate strategy to use.

When hatching activity is nonexistent, anglers should focus their attention upon the larval stage. Anglers should first concentrate their efforts on the shallow portions of a pond or lake. Areas with rocks, logs, or weeds often harbor large numbers of cased caddis and are excellent places to begin probing the water.

Anglers can choose between two methods when presenting cased caddis imitations. One method involves fishing from a watercraft, while the other method involves fishing from shore or wading.

When fly fishing from a watercraft, anglers should cast as close to shore as possible. Again, areas that have large numbers of cased caddis should receive highest priority. After the fly has settled to the bottom, a very slow hand-twist retrieve should be used. Because the fly should be crawled along the bottom where it will remain in the proper feeding zone, a uniform sinking line is an excellent choice. Once the fly has been retrieved through the littoral zone, the angler can begin the next cast.

The second approach is for wading or shoreline anglers. A uniform sinking line again should be the anglers first choice because it will allow the fly to stay along the bottom the entire length of the retrieve as it moves from deep to shallow water. An angler can employ a very slow draw or use the hand-twist retrieve. Perhaps, this method is the most effective of the two because the level at which the fly travels can be controlled the whole way.

It is during periods when caddisflies emerge that anglers should focus on pupa imitations and their associated strategies. When they are making their ascent toward the surface or while they are moving about under the surface of a pond or lake, trout will consume large quantities of caddis pupae. The observant fly angler in the right place at the right time may have some exciting action for trout that are keyed in on this important food source.

Although the angler may never see them ascending toward the surface, a telltale sign that caddisfly pupae are emerging is the presence of the first few adults floating upon the surface. Before large quantities of adult caddisflies are available to feeding trout, the fly angler should try a couple of strategies for presenting pupa imitations.

The first technique should imitate a caddisfly pupa's ascent toward the surface. A Deep Sparkle Pupa is an excellent pattern to begin probing the water with. The best way to imitate an ascending pupa is to allow the fly to reach the bottom, then slowly draw the line in with a steady retrieve until it reaches the surface. Caddis pupae are fairly strong swimmers. Thus, no hesitations should be made during the retrieve. The angler should watch for strikes at any time during the retrieve. Often the most startling strikes will occur at the surface when least expected. At times, a vicious strike will result in the departure of the fly.

If the above strategy proves to be ineffective, the fly angler should present a pupa imitation just below the surface. The fly can either be allowed to drift naturally or an occasional twitch of the rod tip can be imparted. This technique is generally most effective when large numbers of caddis pupae have amassed under the surface.

The leaping and slashing of large trout after adult caddisflies floating or skating upon the surface can stir up quite a bit of excitement in even the most seasoned fly angler. With shaking hands, many an angler has fumbled about trying to tie on an adult caddis imitation. However, once the angler gains composure, two very simplistic techniques can be employed.

The first strategy focuses on a trout's instinct to attack a struggling insect. By imparting an occasional twitch to the rod tip, an angler will often elicit a strike from a trout that is unwilling to take a dead drifted pupa or adult imitation. An Elk Hair Caddis works very nicely in this case due to its floatability.

Another tactic involves skating the fly across the surface. Trout cruising near the surface will often crush the fly when presented in this manner. The angler should make sure the fly is well coated with fly floatant before skating it across the surface or it may sink and become unproductive.

Females returning to the water to lay their eggs present yet another opportunity for the fly angler to cash in on caddisfly activity. The majority of the caddisfly species lay their eggs upon the surface where the eggs then descend gradually to the bottom, while a few species have the characteristic of diving into the water and swimming directly to the bottom to lay their eggs.

Depending on the species present in a pond or lake, an angler will have to choose between presenting the fly upon or below the surface. The techniques mentioned above for presenting adult imitations will also work for imitating egg laying females upon the surface. When imitating caddisfly species that lay their eggs below the surface, some anglers prefer to place a splitshot on the head of an adult imitation such as a Diving Caddis while still other fly anglers will use a weighted pupa imitation with the sink and draw technique.

Like so many other insects available to trout, the angler will have to determine the stage at which trout are feeding on caddisflies. There will be times when this can be quite exasperating, but in the long run the dedicated, inquisitive fly angler will unravel many hidden secrets yet to be discovered.

WATER BOATMEN

The water boatmen is an interesting little bug of the order Hemiptera. With its legs set outward, the water boatmen looks like a boat with oars. It is a brisk, little swimmer and can often be seen scurrying about in the shallows of ponds and lakes.

Water boatmen generally have a mottled olive or brown back with a pale yellow or white underside. Although there is some variance in size among species, most water boatmen never exceed one-half inch in length.

Because of its need for oxygen, the water boatmen must come to the surface to capture an air bubble. Once it collects a bubble, the boatmen then scurries downward. In between each trip to the surface, the boatmen must spend most of its time looking for food. Due to being quite buoyant, the boatmen must attach itself to the bottom or vegetation when at rest.

The water boatmen along with its cousin the backswimmer have a beetle-like appearance because of their flattened bodies. The two, however, are quite easily distinguished from one another by observing their swimming styles. The backswimmer as its name suggests swims upside down, whereas the boatmen swims right side up.

During the mating season, water boatmen leave the water. Depending on the species, this can take place in spring or fall. Upon reentering the water after mating, water boatmen make quite a splash. At this time, trout have been known to feed quite ravenously on them. An angler that is present when this occurs and realizes what is happening can have a field day with gluttonous trout.

FLY FISHING STRATEGIES

Fly anglers imitating water boatmen should concentrate on their movements and behavior. This means that presentations will usually be made to shallow water while incorporating the erratic movements of the boatmen during the retrieve.

With most casts being made to shallow water, a long leader tapered to 6X or 7X is a necessity. A Prince Nymph or Water Boatman weighted towards the front will give the angler a presentable imitation to work with.

Again, the angler should cast to shallow areas near submerged weedbeds or logs. The fly should be allowed to reach the bottom before starting the retrieve. With a weighted fly, this will not take very long. When retrieving the fly, use a pulsating motion with the rod that will mimic the darting movements of the boatmen as it ascends toward the surface. This can be done throughout the entire retrieve, or the angler can allow a short pause now and then to let the fly sink before continuing the retrieve.

Another strategy involves imitating the behavior of an egg laying female returning to the water. Of course, an angler will have to be lucky enough to be on the water when this occurs. An unweighted Water Boatman or Prince Nymph with a little fly floatant can be the ticket to success at this time. By presenting the fly with an occasional twitch, the angler will effectively imitate the boatmen's attempt to break through the surface. Trout feeding on water boatmen trying to reenter a pond or lake will have trouble resisting an imitation presented in this manner.

LEECHES

Negative connotations have generally been associated with leeches due to a few species having the habit of drawing blood from humans when attached for prolonged periods of time. However, the majority of leech species are quite harmless to humans and provide a valuable food source for trout in ponds and lakes.

Leeches are annelid worms of the order Hirudinea. They are easy to recognize due to their round, sucking mouth part and flattened body, which moves slowly through the water in a steady, undulating motion.

Most leeches range in length from one to six inches, although they usually average two to three inches. Depending on the species, coloration will vary in ponds and lakes with black, olive, and brown being most common. Leeches are generally lighter on their undersides with some species having spots, stripes, or mottled markings.

Leeches are nocturnal for the most part preferring to move about under the cover of darkness. Dark ponds and lakes seem to harbor the largest populations of leeches, especially those waters with mucky bottoms containing masses of dead organisms and vegetation. Anglers should be aware of these tendencies when choosing to imitate leeches.

FLY FISHING STRATEGIES

Trout will often consume leeches when other food sources are scarce in ponds and lakes. Smaller leeches seem to be preferred by trout over larger ones. In fact, it is rare to find a large number of 5- to 6-inch leeches in the stomachs of trout.

Leeches tend to be found in and around vegetation and logs. Therefore, it is best to begin your search in shallow areas of a pond or lake with weedbeds, brushpiles, and log cribs. Areas around inlets and outlets where woody debris has accumulated are especially good starting points.

When making a presentation, fly anglers should try to simulate the slow, undulating motion of a leech moving through the water. The Woolly Bugger with its enticing marabou tail is an excellent pattern to begin with. The fly should always be allowed to reach the bottom before making a retrieve. This may lead to a few hang-ups, but the angler will also experience more action near the bottom with a leech imitation.

A simple hand-twist retrieve mixed with a slow, steady strip will give the marabou tail of the Woolly Bugger a pulsating motion that often entices even the most lethargic trout. However, the fly angler will have to determine the correct time to strike depending on how hard trout are hitting on any particular day. Often, when trout are hitting lightly, the angler will have to hesitate a second before setting the hook. Only experimentation and time on the water will help an angler increase his/her hooking rate.

SPIN FISHING STRATEGIES

Spin anglers spend the majority of their time on the water casting lures that imitate forage fish. In general, these lures are very effective and have produced some extremely large trout. However, on waters that are designated as artificial lures only, trout become quite shy of spinners and spoons when seen on a daily basis.

Therefore, ponds and lakes with special regulations are ideal waters to begin experimenting with lures that imitate leeches. In particular, spin anglers should focus on ponds and lakes that have mucky bottoms. Weighted jigs designed with marabou tails are excellent leech imitations. Black jigs in the one- to two-inch category seem to produce the best results.

Anglers should begin working the shallow areas of a pond or lake that have a mix of weeds and logs. Jigs should always be allowed to sink completely to the bottom before they are retrieved. This may result in a few lost lures, but the rewards should be worth the effort.

Initially, a sharp twitch should be given to the rod tip to lift the jig quickly from the bottom. This often stirs up a little cloud of sediment and sometimes draws a quick strike from a trout nearby. If a strike is not forthcoming, the angler should then impart action to the jig by slowly pumping the rod while continuously retrieving line. This seems to work better than a steady retrieve with no action imparted at all. In deep water, this method is also productive as is vertical jigging. Vertical jigging, however, requires intense concentration and very quick reflexes and for the most part can be quite boring.

MAYFLIES

Mayflies ranging in size from tiny *Tricorythodes* to giant *Hexagenias* can be found in large numbers throughout Michigan. By comparison, mayfly species are much more widely distributed in Michigan trout streams than in trout ponds and lakes. Of the mayflies available in Michigan's stillwaters, *Hexagenia Limbata* is the most important species for trout as a food source.

The nymph of the *Hexagenia* mayfly is well known to bait fishers as they are commonly sold in bait shops in spring and early summer. Except during emergence, Hex nymphs are usually not visible to anglers because they burrow into silt and sand. However, under the cover of darkness Hex nymphs will leave their burrows for short periods of time. Right before emergence takes place their movements will generally become even greater.

The Hex hatch takes place in most parts of the U.P. in June or early July. As the days become warmer and longer, Hex nymphs will begin to emerge in most ponds and lakes at twilight or shortly thereafter. They are strong swimmers and move in a hinge-like manner towards the surface.

Once they reach the surface, mayfly nymphs split their shucks and emerge as duns. These miniature sailboats riding upon the surface are highly visible to trout on the prowl. Duns are consumed in large numbers by ravenous trout as they dry their wings before taking flight.

When their wings have finally dried enough, duns will fly to nearby vegetation along the shoreline of a pond or lake. Depending upon weather conditions, duns may lie dormant for a few days. Once they shed their outer skins, mayflies are known as spinners. At this stage of life, they are now ready to mate.

After mating takes place, females will fly over the surface of the water and deposit their eggs. Females will then fall into the water and lie spent upon the surface. This, in turn, may cause another feeding frenzy if spent mayflies are available in large numbers.

FLY FISHING STRATEGIES

Many trout ponds and lakes throughout the U.P. become exciting waters to cast a fly upon during the giant *Hexagenia* mayfly hatch. At this time of the trout season, fly anglers have perhaps their best chance to land a trophy brookie in the 3- to 5-pound class.

When chasing the Hex hatch, timing is everything. Water temperature often plays a central role in determining when a hatch will occur on a given water. Anglers should also keep in mind that hatches in the northern most parts of the U.P. start two to three weeks later than the southern U.P. and lower Michigan. Therefore, when planning a trip to a particular part of the U.P. in search of mayfly slurping brookies, call ahead to find out if the hatch has begun.

During the beginning of the emergence phase, a Woolly Bugger or Hex nymph pattern fished on a deep line will often produce trout in the early evening hours to twilight. When imitating a Hex nymph, anglers should always allow the fly to reach bottom before starting a retrieve. Line should then be retrieved with a steady strip and an occasional twitch of the rod tip. This will simulate the hinge-like movement of a Hex nymph as it ascends toward the surface. Once the fly reaches the surface, it should be twitched along the surface to imitate a nymph trying to break out of its shuck.

When duns appear around dusk, fly anglers should change their tactics from subsurface to surface. At this time, anglers will need to switch from a nymph to a dun pattern. Making this switch can be quite difficult in the gathering darkness if the angler has not come prepared with a flashlight.

Although a small flashlight is an invaluable tool, anglers should make sure they keep the light off the water where trout are feeding to prevent spooking them.

During the hatch, anglers should try to cast to trout that are feeding nearby. Occasionally, a trout may be feeding continuously and will be an easy target. Anglers should remember it is always easier to hook a fish within sight when fishing in the dark. If a splash or slurp occurs close to where you think the fly has landed but out of sight, an angler should strike very gently. More often than not when striking by sound alone the angler will come up empty handed. However, there is always that chance that the next strike may be a trophy, so keep your eyes and ears focused. A Hex hatch will vary greatly depending upon weather conditions, but these moments may be the most exciting and intense of the season.

Once their wings are sufficiently dried, duns will fly off to nearby vegetation and buildings. During this brief stage of life, duns will shed their outer skins. Mayflies are known as spinners now and begin to mate. Females will then fly over the surface of the water and deposit their eggs. Shortly thereafter, they will begin to die. Many females will fall spent upon the surface. Fly anglers on the water during a spinner fall will need to tie on a spentwing imitation to entice trout feeding on the mayflies grand finale.

SPIN FISHING STRATEGIES

Most spin anglers would declare that a mayfly hatch marks the end of their fishing for a while. However, some lures have been designed in recent years that at least make an attempt to match the hatch. Generally, these lures are most effective during emergence and best imitate an emerging nymph. The Thunder Bug developed by Mepps does a nice job imitating mayfly and caddisfly nymphs.

When fishing a lure like a Thunder Bug, spin anglers should start with a very slow retrieve. Again it is best to focus on that time right before dusk when nymphs are emerging. A very light line retrieved with a slight twitch of the rod tip will help the lure work much more effectively and will give the lure a pulsating, lifelike movement that resembles a swimming Hex nymph. Try the same technique during caddisfly and dragonfly hatches. The results may amaze the dedicated spin angler.

TERRESTRIALS

Terrestrial insects are not often thought of as a food source for stillwater trout. The fact is terrestrials can be found at certain times of the year in large numbers upon the surfaces of ponds and lakes. Due to heavy winds, driving rainstorms, and poorly navigated flights, many terrestrials land in ponds and lakes inadvertently.

The most important terrestrial insects of interest to fly anglers are ants and beetles. During exceptionally large hatches, flying ants can be found in extremely large numbers on land and in the water. Swarms of flying ants are often blown to the windward side of a lake where opportunistic trout prey heavily upon them. When flying ants are present in such large numbers, fly anglers should be sure to check out this side of the lake. A black flying ant pattern fished on a long leader is usually the most effective way to entice trout during a large hatch.

Beetles are also found during the summer months along the edges of stillwaters. These insects often fall into the water in large quantities due to the same reasons mentioned above for flying ants. When a large number of beetles are available, trout will feed quite heavily on these high protein treats. Fly anglers that are aware of beetle activity along the shoreline can have a field day hooking aggressive trout in very shallow water. Various beetle patterns are available to the angler with black being the most productive color. Again, a long, fine leader should be used when working the shallowest parts of a lake.

CHAPTER 7

A SELECTION OF TROUT PONDS AND LAKES

With so many ponds and lakes to choose from throughout the Upper Peninsula of Michigan, it is very difficult to select a sample of stillwaters containing trout. The ponds and lakes presented in this chapter are but a fraction of those waters available to the adventurous trout angler and only serve as a springboard for those that are interested in sampling some of the backwoods trout waters available in the U.P. of Michigan. For those that become hooked on stillwater trout fishing there is a large listing of trout ponds and lakes throughout the entire Upper Peninsula to choose from in the next chapter. Most of these ponds and lakes are designated trout waters that receive plantings of trout on a yearly basis.

Trout ponds and lakes profiled in this chapter for the most part are also designated trout waters, which the DNR stocks and manages for trout only. However, a few may contain warmwater species besides trout. Naturally reproducing populations of brook trout are not present in the majority of these waters. Thus, trout anglers interested in this aspect of the stillwater trout fishery in the U.P. will need to locate these unnamed spring ponds and lakes on their own.

Each trout pond or lake is presented with a simple locator map. These maps show the contour of each pond or lake along with any inlets, outlets, or springs that may be present. Trails and roads, which may or may not be named, are also shown on each map so anglers can see how accessible a pond or lake may be. These simple maps should be used in conjunction with county and quadrangle maps, which are much better tools for locating a given pond or lake. Maximum depths and acreage of a pond or lake are also shown on each map to give the trout angler a feel for the size of the water.

A short overview of the ponds and lakes in this chapter accompany each locator map. These discussions should help the angler get a better picture of the area encompassing each water. Trout stockings that have taken place recently are also mentioned with reference to the species and strain of trout and the number of trout that are planted on a regular basis. A brief comment about the communities, attractions, and resources available near these waters is also provided. Hopefully, these notes will help the visiting angler plan a successful trip to the Upper Peninsula in search of stillwater trout.

ADDIS LAKES
ALGER COUNTY

Addis Lakes I
Area: 7.0 Acres
Maximum Depth: 15 Feet
Addis Lakes II
Area: 3.75 Acres
Maximum Depth: 5 Feet

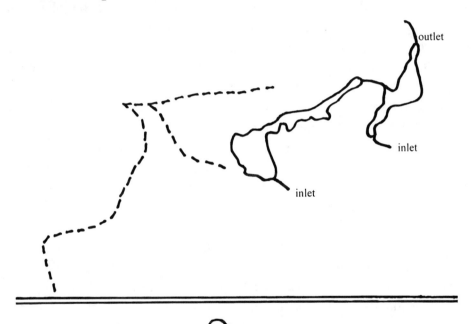

ADDIS LAKES I AND II
ALGER COUNTY

Lying just north of Hwy. 94 between Munising and Chatham, Addis Lakes I and II form the headwaters of Addis Creek, which flows in a northerly direction to Au Train Lake. These lakes are hidden away at the end of a complex of rugged backroads in the heart of the Hiawatha National Forest. Due to deep ruts in these two-tracks, a four wheel drive vehicle is recommended, especially during the early part of the trout season.

Once the angler arrives at the upper lake, it is only a short portage down a small hill to the water's edge. On dry land above the lake, some anglers prefer to pitch a tent and make camp for a night or two. The shoreline of this lake is somewhat marshy. Thus, in an effort to stay dry anglers may want to bring along a pair of hip boots during the wettest part of the season. Those anglers that are interested in wildlife will often see beaver and heron around or in the lake to add to the enjoyment of their trip.

Addis Lake I is the deepest and most productive of the two lakes with a maximum depth of 15 feet near the upper end. The upper end is shaped like a bowl with the tail end being much narrower and shallower. Most anglers definitely prefer to probe the deeper water during the summer. However, the lower end leading to the outlet can be productive early and late in the season.

Like the majority of trout ponds and lakes in Alger County, Addis Lakes I and II are stocked with brook trout. Most recently, the lakes have been stocked with the Temiscamie strain of brook trout, which is an import from Canada. The Assinica strain, which is another Canadian brook trout strain, has also been stocked during the 1990s. In most years, these lakes have received 900 to 1050 brookies averaging five inches in length. Both strains of brook trout have exceptional growth rates and put on weight once they reach 12 to 14 inches in length.

The Hiawatha National Forest is a beautiful area to visit and also a refreshing place to just hang out and camp for a few days. If you don't prefer camping, the city of Munising, known as the place of the island, is an excellent location to make your headquarters while on a trout fishing trip. While visiting the Munising area, the trout angler should definitely make it a point to see Pictured Rocks National Lakeshore and several gorgeous waterfalls right outside the city limits.

COLE CREEK POND
ALGER COUNTY

Cole Creek Pond
Area: 5.0 Acres
Maximum Depth: 4 feet

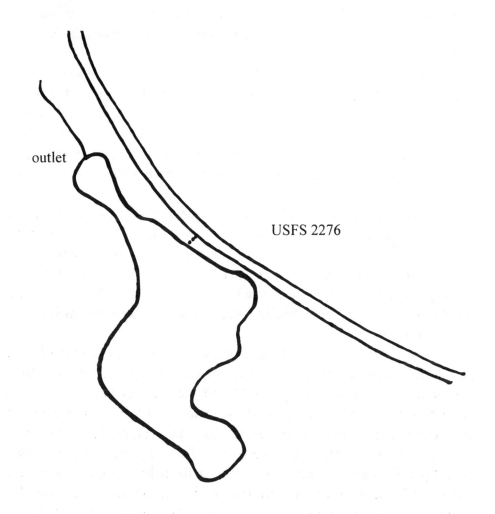

outlet

USFS 2276

COLE CREEK POND
ALGER COUNTY

Cole Creek Pond is a small, nondescript body of water that lies nearly equidistantly between Au Train and Munising in the Hiawatha National Forest. This little five-acre pond forms the headwaters of Cole Creek, which trickles in a northwesterly direction to Au Train Lake. Beavers have been active in this area for many years and have placed a stable dam across the outlet. Because this fishery relies solely on stocked trout, this beaver dam appears to pose no harm to the trout population of Cole Creek Pond.

Reaching Cole Creek Pond is fairly easy off Forest Road 2276. A small pulloff area is available to anglers with a short portage to the boggy shoreline of this small pond. Anglers should be sure to watch their step as they approach the edge of the pond, because the muck is very thick. In fact, nearly the entire bottom of Cole Creek Pond is composed of muck and marl. This makes a canoe a necessity as wading is definitely out of the question.

Near the landing anglers will find many old stumps imbedded in the muck. The area around these stumps is rather shallow and unproductive. Lily pads are also present in this area and trout can be found in and around them. *Chara* is the number one weed present in this pond and large numbers of aquatic invertebrates live in these weed masses. There are large, mucky springfed openings within these weedbeds where the majority of trout can be found.

Generally, Cole Creek Pond has received 600 brookies in the 5-inch range. Both Temiscamie and Assinica strains of brook trout have been planted in this pond in recent years. Growth rates appear to be excellent as these brookies do take advantage of the multitudes of chubs and dace that are present along with the ever present scuds and midges. Brook trout that survive a few years in this pond are quite bulky and provide anglers with a good fight. On overcast days and during twilight hours, smaller brookies can often be seen feeding on prolific midge hatches over the springfed openings. These underlings can provide some fast and fun dry fly fishing.

Cole Creek Pond is an excellent choice for the catch and release angler with the majority of brookies measuring less than 10 inches in length. The knowledgable angler may, however, be able to tie into one or two of the leviathans that are present within this pond.

Anglers can take advantage of the campgrounds present within the majestic Hiawatha National Forest or as mentioned before enjoy the amenities found within the picturesque city of Munising. Make sure you take some time during your trip to Alger County to sample a pasty or two along with some freshly smoked Lake Superior lake trout and whitefish. These are both U.P. delicacies you just can't pass up.

WEST TROUT LAKE POND
ALGER COUNTY

West Trout Lake Pond
Area: 8.5 Acres
Maximum Depth: 10 feet

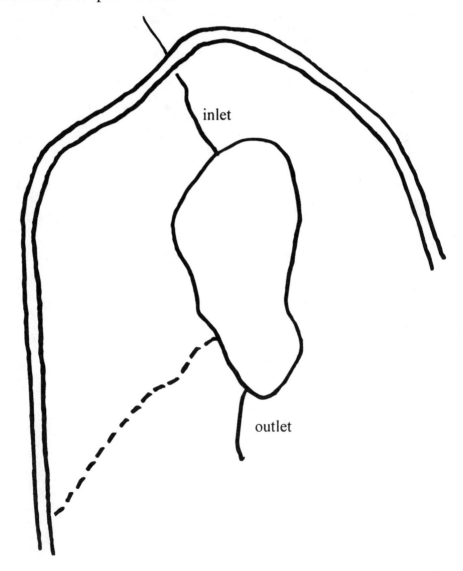

inlet

outlet

WEST TROUT LAKE POND
ALGER COUNTY

West Trout Lake Pond is an 8.5-acre spring pond that is connected to Trout Lake via its outlet. Trout Lake is a long 42-acre body of water with many springs entering along its entire length. This whole system is well known for its terrific brook trout fishing. To supplement the wild trout fishery, several thousand brookies are planted in selected parts of Trout Lake on a yearly basis.

This spring pond along with Trout Lake and its feeders is located just south of the Cleveland Cliff Basin and east of the small communities of Traunik and Trenary. This complex of trout waters forms the headwaters of the East Branch of the Whitefish River, which has several beautiful miles of brook trout water. Several trout streams and spring ponds feeding into this system also contain brook trout, which makes this area one of the premier trout fishing regions in the Upper Peninsula.

For trout anglers interested in wild brook trout, West Trout Lake Pond is an excellent choice to begin with. This pond is a prime example of a quality spring pond. Cold, spring inflows are present nearly everywhere including deep springs in the upper end of the pond. Sufficient space for spawning is also present to sustain a quality trout fishery, although stocked trout may be present via its outlet to Trout Lake.

Wild brook trout fisheries such as West Trout Lake Pond should be treated with the utmost respect. Therefore, to ensure that West Trout Lake Pond and other wild brook trout fisheries are saved for future generations, anglers should limit their kill and not kill their limit.

Trout anglers planning a trip to this part of the Hiawatha National Forest could spend a whole month fishing and still cover only a fraction of the trout resources available. Again, visiting anglers can take advantage of the campgrounds present in the Hiawatha or perhaps rent a cabin at one of the resorts in the Au Train area. Munising is also only a short jaunt away and offers many attractions for the whole family.

NAOMIKONG LAKE
CHIPPEWA COUNTY

Naomikong Lake
Area: 13.9 Acres
Maximum Depth: 5 feet

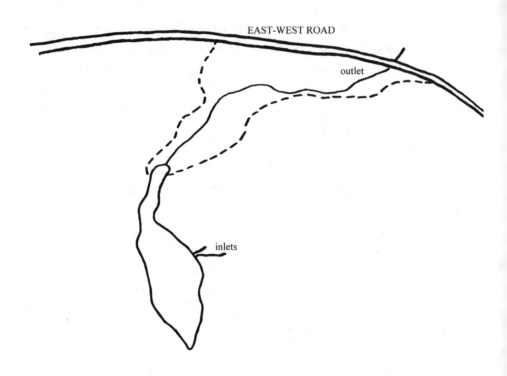

NAOMIKONG LAKE
CHIPPEWA COUNTY

Naomikong Lake rises out of a swampy area just a little over a mile south of the shores of Lake Superior. Its outlet, Naomikong Creek, winds in a northerly direction mostly through the Hiawatha National Forest and empties into Tahquamenon Bay. This 14-acre lake is actually a large spring pond with spring inlets entering on the south and east sides of the lake. Although its maximum depth is only approximately five feet, Naomikong Lake does offer a viable trout fishery.

Anglers can reach Naomikong Lake by taking the East and West Road off Lakeshore Drive. Naomikong Lake is not far from the beaten path but far enough removed to be passed over by trout anglers in search of stream trout in the East Branch of the Tahquamenon River and other trout creeks in the vicinity.

With its irregular shoreline, Naomikong Lake is biologically quite productive. Three-inch brook trout fingerlings that are planted each spring grow to regulation size in about two to three years. Recently, the DNR has been stocking the lake with the Temiscamie strain of brook trout and an Assinica/Maine cross. Due to the fact that so many small brookies are present in the population each year, trout anglers should use artificial lures or flies. Survival of these small trout is much higher when using an artificial lure or fly.

Those parts of the lake that receive spring inflows throughout the season are the most productive areas during the summer. Brook trout tend to stay near these inflows wherever cover such as weedbeds and logs are present.

A wide variety of food sources are present in Naomikong Lake and can be imitated by both the fly and spin angler. Be sure to take some time to study the surface and air to see if any insect activity is occurring. If there is a large hatch occurring, an angler should use the proper imitations and strategies presented earlier in this book. Probing the water with a nymph or streamer can be effective for the fly fisher when hatches are not occurring, while a small aglia spinner can be productive for the spin angler.

Many outdoor attractions await the visiting angler in this section of Chippewa County. Tahquamenon Falls and Whitefish Point are two scenic places the angler may want to visit. Tahquamenon Falls is approximately 200 feet wide with a 50-foot drop. Nearly 500,000 people visit this majestic waterfall annually. Whitefish Point is home to the Great Lakes Shipwreck Museum and is also located near the area where the Edmund Fitzgerald sank. Eckerman, which is a small community south of Naomikong Lake, should also be mentioned due to the restaurants and lodging this village has to offer to the traveling angler.

ROXBURY POND NO. 1
CHIPPEWA COUNTY

Roxbury Pond No. 1
Area: 9.8 Acres
Maximum Depth: 10 feet

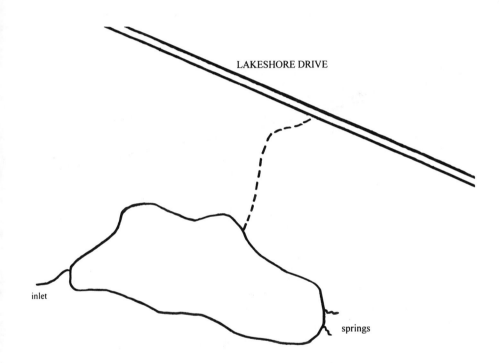

ROXBURY POND NO. 2
CHIPPEWA COUNTY

Roxbury Pond No. 2
Area: 3.7 Acres
Maximum Depth: 5 feet

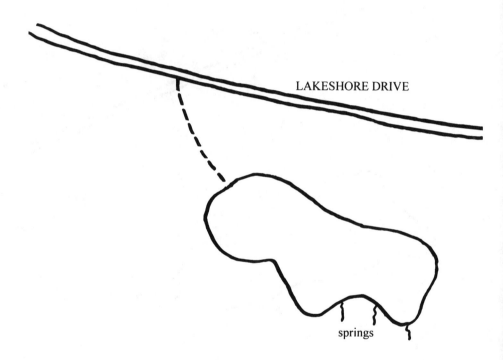

LAKESHORE DRIVE

springs

ROXBURY PONDS 1 AND 2
CHIPPEWA COUNTY

The Roxbury Ponds were created when two borrow pits filled in with water. These pits were dug in an area near Lake Superior where Roxbury Creek enters the big lake, Gitchee Gumee. In essence these two ponds are now trout waters because they were dug in areas with vast quantities of groundwater. With spring inflows present, brook trout were the natural choice for stocking in these ponds.

Anglers traveling on Lakeshore Drive can find these ponds just south of the road in the vicinity of Roxbury Creek. Roxbury Pond 1 lies on the west side of the creek and has a surface area of approximately 10 acres. Roxbury Pond 2 can be found just east of the creek and is about 4 acres in size. Both ponds are very accessible. Several other trout waters, however, can be found in this part of Chippewa County and may reduce the number of anglers using these ponds. For example, Roxbury Creek is right next door and provides some excellent fishing for wild brook trout.

Brook trout averaging three to five inches in length have been stocked annually in the Roxbury Ponds. Generally, Roxbury Pond 1 has received 800 to 1000 brook trout, while Roxbury Pond 2 is planted with about 300 fingerlings. Different strains of brook trout including the Temiscamie and Assinica have been planted in recent years. Because there are so many sublegal trout present in the Roxbury Ponds each year, anglers should use artificial flies and lures. Releasing small trout properly is essential to the future of any trout fishery.

With such a large number of trout waters present in this area, visiting anglers will have a nice selection of waters to choose from. The attractions and accommodations mentioned in the Naomikong Lake section should also be considered by traveling anglers visiting the Roxbury Ponds.

CORNELIA LAKE
GOGEBIC COUNTY

Cornelia Lake
Area: 14.1 Acre
Maximum Depth: 38 feet

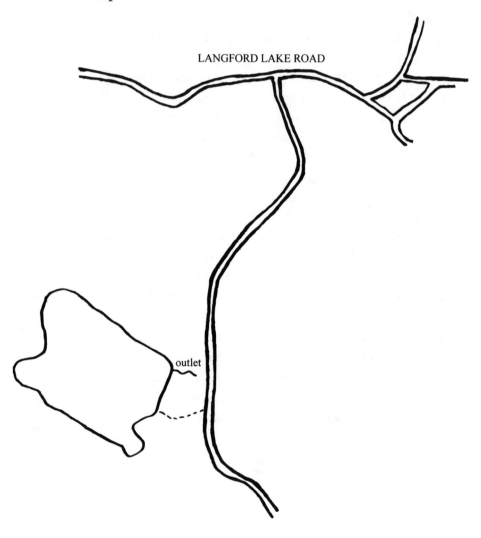

CORNELIA LAKE
GOGEBIC COUNTY

Cornelia Lake is part of the Ottawa National Forest and is located several miles southwest of Watersmeet. This 14-acre bog lake is one of the many small lakes to be found in this part of the Ottawa National Forest. During the summer, this swampy area plays host to swarms of mosquitoes and noseeums. These nasty pests make insect repellent a necessity for the trout angler, especially on warm, humid evenings.

Anglers driving west of Watersmeet on US Highway 2 can reach Cornelia Lake by taking the forest service road south off Langford Lake Road. For the most part, the forest service roads in this area are well maintained and anglers should have no difficulty reaching this lake.

The outline of Cornelia Lake is somewhat smooth with only a couple of indentations. There are two deep holes that reach over 30 feet in depth. Along the southern most part of the lake there is a steep dropoff that extends out to one of the deepest parts of the lake. This dropoff and the area straight out from the landing can be highly productive places to fish for trout during the summer.

Cornelia Lake is a designated trout lake that is managed solely for brook trout. In recent years, the lake has received the Assinica strain and an Assinica/Maine cross. Plantings of seven-inch brook trout have ranged in number from 800 to 1100. Trout residing in the lake for a year should generally reach the legal size limit of 10 inches.

Campgrounds are available nearby on Langford and Pomeroy Lakes and are maintained by the United States Forest Service. Resorts are also plentiful on large lakes in Gogebic County and in Vilas County just across the border in Wisconsin. A motel is available for weary travelers in Watersmeet along with a few restaurants.

Trout anglers visiting this part of the Ottawa National Forest may want to spend a day or two fishing on the Middle Branch of the Ontonagon River above and below Watersmeet. The river below Bond Falls has provided excellent trout fishing in the past and is frequented yearly by anglers from all over the United States. Bond Falls is a beautiful place to take the entire family and enjoy a picnic lunch while listening to the roar of the falls in the background. Campsites are available on Bond Falls Flowage and anglers can try their hand at fishing for many warmwater species that are found in the flowage.

LITTLE DUCK LAKE
GOGEBIC COUNTY

Little Duck Lake
Area: 42 Acre
Maximum Depth: 69 feet

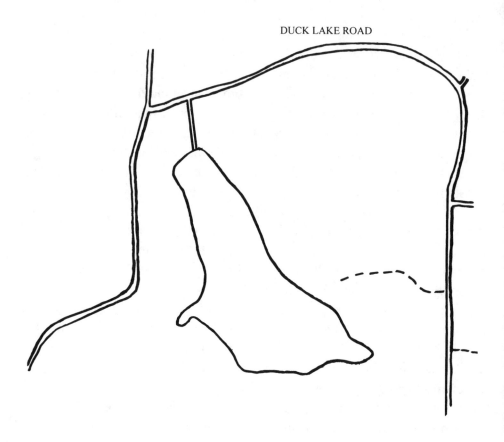

DUCK LAKE ROAD

LITTLE DUCK LAKE
GOGEBIC COUNTY

A short drive south of Watersmeet on US Highway 45 and then west on county and forest service roads will take the angler to the landing on the north end of Little Duck Lake. Acrobatic rainbows along with splake await the trout angler that chooses to cast a line on this 42-acre lake.

Little Duck Lake is larger than the average trout pond or lake in the Upper Peninsula and provides a two-story fishery during the summer. This lake has two deep holes with the upper one extending down to a depth of nearly 70 feet. There are steep dropoffs on the east and west sides of this hole, which hold quite a few trout. Deadfalls litter the shoreline and provide plenty of cover for trout early and late in the season. Gravel bottoms are also found in a few areas around the lake.

Rainbow trout of the California Shasta strain along with the brook/lake trout cross known as splake have been stocked in recent years. Generally, 3000 seven- to eight-inch rainbow trout have been planted annually. This particular strain of rainbow grows rather quickly and may reach 12 to 14 inches a year after being stocked. Splake, which prefer colder water temperatures than rainbows, are stocked at a rate of 1200 to 1500 per year and for the most part are fished for with bait over deep water.

During the warmest part of the summer, rainbow trout and splake take up residency in the coldwater column of this lake. Although the depth of this water favors the spin angler, fly fishers will find plenty of action early and late in the season near shore and also in open water during midge, caddisfly, and mayfly hatches when proper water temperatures exist.

Trout fishers that prefer fishing for stillwater rainbows will enjoy the time they spend fishing on Little Duck Lake. However, other fishing opportunities are also available to the angler in this part of Gogebic County. When visiting this part of the Ottawa National Forest, anglers should take a day to sample the superb trout fishing on the various branches of the Ontonagon River along with their feeder creeks. The Sylvania Recreation Area also beckons the adventurous canoer and camper to spend a few days in the backcountry of the Upper Peninsula. This area provides some excellent smallmouth bass fishing. Anglers, however, must use artificial lures and release all bass immediately.

Again, anglers can take advantage of the many campgrounds that exist in the Ottawa National Forest or spend a night or two in a motel in Watersmeet or Land O' Lakes, Wisconsin. For those anglers that enjoy gambling, there is a brand new casino just north of Watersmeet. This casino is owned and managed by the Lac Vieux Desert Indian tribe and has lodging and dining facilities. The historic Gateway Inn in Land O' Lakes also provides lodging for the visiting angler and has a restaurant and gift shop attached to the building.

MISHIKE LAKE
GOGEBIC COUNTY

Mishike Lake
Area: 15 Acre
Maximum Depth: 30 feet

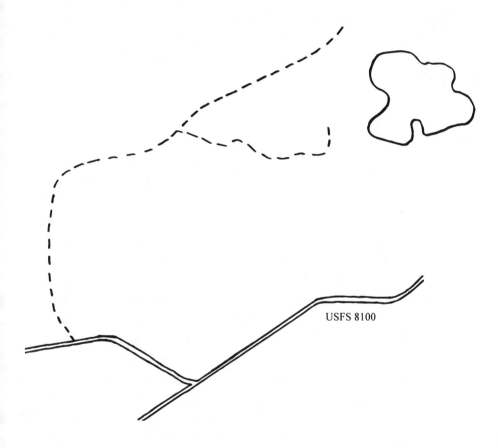

USFS 8100

MISHIKE LAKE
GOGEBIC COUNTY

Mishike Lake lies on the western fringe of the Ottawa National Forest at the end of an old logging road. This 15-acre lake has an irregular shoreline with steep dropoffs occurring wherever points jut out into the lake. Nearly half of the shoreline has an encroaching bog. Steep slopes exist along the east and south sides of the lake. During the summer, large weedbeds extend out to 12 feet of water.

Anglers can reach Mishike Lake by traveling west on Forest Service Road 8100 off of State Highway 64 south of Marenisco. After passing Plymouth Lake, there will be a curve to the right and anglers must then take an unmarked logging road also to the right and follow this until it deadends. There is a small parking area at the end of the trail and a very short portage to the lake.

Mishike Lake is managed for brook trout only and receives approximately 700 brook trout of the Assinica strain on a yearly basis. Brook trout that are stocked in this lake generally average around seven inches in length and reach regulation size in a year.

Anglers fishing from a canoe or small boat can cover Mishike Lake quite thoroughly. The area straight out from the landing along with the dropoffs around the points on the east and south shores of the lake can be very productive for the trout angler early in the season. During the summer, anglers should move out to the deepest edges of these dropoffs as trout move to these depths for the colder water temperatures that prevail in these areas.

Designated trout lakes are only a small part of the fishery in Gogebic County. This county, due to the variety of waters that exist, has perhaps the most varied fishery in the state. Therefore, anglers may wish to sample some bass, walleye, northern, and musky fishing while in the area. Again, anglers can take advantage of the same accommodations mentioned under the Little Duck Lake section.

PLYMOUTH LAKE
GOGEBIC COUNTY

Plymouth Lake
Area: 27.5 Acre
Maximum Depth: 15 feet

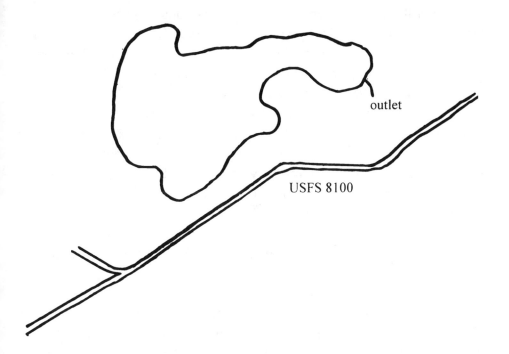

outlet

USFS 8100

PLYMOUTH LAKE
GOGEBIC COUNTY

As noted in the Mishike Lake section, Forest Service Road 8100 skirts the edge of Plymouth Lake. This forest service road is well maintained and there is a pulloff area next to this road overlooking Plymouth Lake that will accommodate three to four vehicles.

This 27-acre lake is surrounded by a beautiful stand of evergreens and hardwoods. In fall, the mixture of the flaming leaves of the hardwoods along with the intense greens of the conifers adds a special touch to the landscape. Plymouth Lake is connected to Taps Lake, which is a small panfish lake, via a very short channel. During the summer, both lakes are overrun with heavy weed growth. In fact, only the middle portion of Plymouth Lake is free of dense weedbeds.

To cover Plymouth Lake effectively, anglers should use a canoe or small boat. Due to the steep approach to the lake, a small canoe would definitely be the most practical choice. Hauling a watercraft back up this steep incline can be very exhausting work, especially when the temperature reaches 80 degrees. Therefore, it is highly recommended that two anglers be present on a fishing excursion to Plymouth Lake.

Warmwater species reside in this lake along with brown trout, which are planted on a yearly basis. Plymouth Lake receives a planting of 1000 brown trout per year. Generally, these browns will average seven inches in length.

Anglers in search of brown trout should focus on the deepest water off the northeast shore before the lake begins to narrow. The steep dropoff that occurs off the southern most point can also be productive for trout at times. If an angler enjoys fishing for panfish, the thick weedbeds in four to five feet of water are generally quite productive.

Time has been kind to this part of Gogebic County as most of the land has remained free of human abuse since the decimation of the great white pine forests. Outdoor enthusiasts that spend a few days in this part of the U.P. will come to appreciate the area that the Chippewa Indians called home so many years ago.

KILLDEER LAKE
IRON COUNTY

Killdeer Lake
Area: 8.4 Acre
Maximum Depth: 45 feet

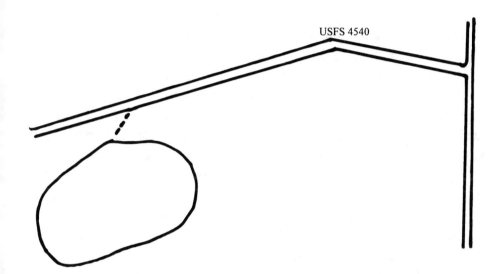

KILLDEER LAKE
IRON COUNTY

The Ottawa National Forest is home to many fine trout waters including Killdeer Lake. This glistening, emerald jewel is one of the many designated trout lakes to be found in western Iron County. Like most designated trout lakes in this part of Iron County, minnows are not allowed as bait on Killdeer Lake. This is undeniably a good law as other managed trout ponds and lakes in the state have been ruined in the past by the introduction of foreign fish species.

Anglers can reach Killdeer Lake through a series of backroads west of Federal Forest Highway 16. There is a small campsite available to anglers along with an outhouse right next to the lake off Forest Road 4540. This recreational area is governed and maintained by the United States Forest Service and anglers are asked to keep this area clean of all trash. There is no sensible reason why anglers should leave a mess behind once they are done fishing. Unfortunately, however, it appears that some anglers have a total disregard for keeping this pristine area clear of litter.

A sandy landing for canoes, float tubes, and small boats is available near the parking area. Besides the landing area, the rest of the shoreline is boggy. Over half the lake is enclosed by steep slopes, which for the most part protect the lake from heavy winds. Although it is fairly round, Killdeer Lake actually has two deep basins. Since these two basins are between 30 to 45 feet deep, brook trout may be difficult to find during the warmest days of summer when they seek cooler water temperatures.

The DNR has stocked Killdeer Lake in the past with Temiscamie, Assinica, and Maine strains of brook trout. Plantings have ranged in number from 800 to 2000 including five-inch fingerlings and adults up to 11 inches. Brook trout growth rates appear to be about average for a pond of this size. Again, trout anglers will have to release all trout under 10 inches in length.

Logs that jut out along the shoreline of this lake provide good cover for trout. Anglers plying the dropoffs near these old, drowned timbers can expect to find good numbers of brook trout, although they may not be the largest in the lake. Small brookies often feed on midges over the entire lake on calm summer evenings. These little brookies sometimes refuse all but the smallest midge imitations. The saddle between the two basins, which is straight out from the landing, can also be productive at times.

If an angler does not wish to camp on the shores of Killdeer Lake, many other accessible campgrounds can be found on larger lakes in the Ottawa National Forest. Many of these lakes provide exceptional fishing for bass, walleye, northerns, and panfish. Also, trout anglers looking for wild trout will find several miles of blue ribbon trout water within the boundaries of the national forest. Noncampers in search of lodging and dining can find everything they are looking for in the city of Iron River along US Highway 2.

SKYLINE LAKE
IRON COUNTY

Skyline Lake
Area: 11.8 Acre
Maximum Depth: 26 feet

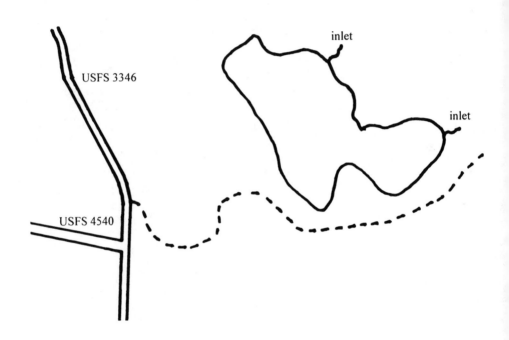

SKYLINE LAKE
IRON COUNTY

Nestled deep in a hollow in the heart of the Ottawa National Forest the area surrounding Skyline Lake appears to have stood still in time. As an angler approaches the boggy shoreline, the eerie tremolo of the loon can often be heard echoing through the pines. This early morning greeting adds a special touch to the stillwater anglers' experience.

Trout anglers can find Skyline Lake by taking Forest Road 3346 north past Forest Road 4540, which runs past Killdeer Lake. The next trail to the right north of Forest Road 4540 leads to Skyline Lake. Portaging in a canoe from the trailhead can be an arduous task for anglers that are not conditioned for such a strenuous hike. Anglers should, therefore, take a casual hike to the lake without any equipment to get a feel for how difficult the terrain may be for them.

Skyline Lake is divided into an east and west basin with the west basin being twice the size of the east basin. Both basins are at least 20 feet deep with plenty of spring feeders to maintain a trout fishery throughout the year. The shoreline surrounding Skyline Lake is boggy, while the bottom of the lake is primarily muck with a small sandy area in the southeast corner. Pond weeds along with lily pads are prevalent in the shallowest areas of the lake. These weedbeds provide a home for numerous aquatic invertebrates.

Brook trout are generally planted on a yearly basis in Skyline Lake. Temiscamie, Assinica, and Maine strains of brook trout have all been stocked in the 1990s. Generally, this lake has received brook trout that average five to six inches in length.

The whole lake can be covered thoroughly by those anglers fishing from a canoe. Anglers should focus first on the steep dropoffs along the southwest shore. A large number of drowned trees provide cover for trout all along this shore. The upper end of the west basin is fed by numerous springs and also holds a good number of brookies.

When visiting this part of Iron County, slow down and take some time to enjoy the beautiful scenery. In a pristine environment such as the Ottawa National Forest, trout fishing can often take a backseat to the peace and solitude that most outdoor enthusiasts crave in this day and age.

CHAPTER 8

A LISTING OF TROUT PONDS AND LAKES

Anglers that are interested in searching out new trout ponds and lakes will find this chapter to be quite valuable. By choosing a county and then searching through the alphabetized listing, an angler will be able to pick a trout pond or lake of interest.

To be sure that a public access exists for a given pond or lake, an angler should refer to a county map. If a county map does not provide enough information on a public access in question, consult an updated county plat book or the nearest DNR district office.

Within this listing, an angler will also find the species of trout present in each pond or lake. Thus, an angler may choose a pond or lake depending on the trout species of greatest appeal.

The majority of the trout ponds and lakes in this listing are stocked with trout, although some of these waters do support wild brook trout. For the adventurous angler interested in native or wild trout there are also plenty of unnamed ponds to explore.

As mentioned earlier in this book, native or wild brook trout populations are generally found in remote spring ponds at the headwaters of small creeks. Due to being remote, most of these ponds have remained nameless. Therefore, an angler will need a good supply of quadrangle maps to locate these remote ponds. Then plan on doing plenty of legwork to reach these glistening gems.

ALGER

NAME	TROUT SPECIES
Addis Lake	Brook
Beanies Pond	Brook
Bette's Pond	Brook
Brian's Pond	Brook
Cheryl's Pond	Brook
Cole Creek Pond	Brook
Grand Marais Lake	Brook
Harrison's Pond	Brook
Hike Lake	Brook
Hyde Lake	Brook
Irwin Lake	Brook, Brown
Juanita Lake	Brown
Kay's Lake	Brook
Legion Lake	Brook
Madison Spring Pond	Brook
Martin's Spring Pond	Brook
Peterson's Spring Pond	Brook
Porter's Pond	Brown
Rock Lake	Brook
Sawaski's Pond	Brook
Seven Mile Lake	Brook
Sullivan Lake	Brook
Trout Lake	Brook
Trout Lake Pond, North	Brook
Trout Lake Pond, West	Brook
Trueman Lake	Brook
Valley Spur Pond	Brook

BARAGA

NAME	TROUT SPECIES
Alberta Pond	Brook
Fence Lake	Rainbow
Roland Pond	Brook

CHIPPEWA

NAME	TROUT SPECIES
Highbanks Lake	Rainbow
Naomikong Lake	Brook
Naomikong Pond	Brook
Roxbury Pond (East)	Brook
Roxbury Pond (West)	Brook
Trout Brook Pond	Brook

DELTA

NAME	TROUT SPECIES
Bear Lake	Brook
Carr Lake	Brook
Kilpecker Pond	Brook
Norway Lake	Brook
Section 1 Pond	Brook
Square Lake	Brook
Wintergreen Lake	Brook
Zigmaul Pond	Brook

DICKINSON

NAME	TROUT SPECIES
Kimberly Clark Pond	Brook

GOGEBIC

NAME	TROUT SPECIES
Beatons Lake	Rainbow
Castle Lake	Brook
Cornelia Lake	Brook
Hilltop Lake	Brook
Little Duck Lake	Brook
Mishike Lake	Brook

Moon Lake	Brown
Paint River Spring Pond	Brook
Plymouth Lake	Brown
Redboat Lake	Brook
Wilson Spring Pond	Brook

HOUGHTON

NAME	TROUT SPECIES
Bass Lake	Brook
Clear Lake	Brook
Crystal Lake	Brown
Emily Lake	Rainbow
Lake on Three	Rainbow
Lower Dam Lake	Brook
Penegore Lake	Brook
Perrault Lake	Brook
Roland Lake	Rainbow

IRON

NAME	TROUT SPECIES
Big Spring Pond	Brook
Caspian Pond	Rainbow
Deadmans Lake	Brook
Fire Lake	Rainbow
Forest Lake	Brook
Fortune Pond	Rainbow
Hannah Webb Lake	Brook, Rainbow
Killdeer Lake	Brook
Long Lake	Rainbow
Madelyn Lake	Brook
Passmore Spring Pond	Brook
Skyline Lake	Brook
Spree Lake	Brook
Timber Lake	Brook

KEWEENAW

NAME	TROUT SPECIES
Bailey Pond	Brook
Lake Desor(Isle Royale)	Brook
Eliza Pond	Brown
Garden City Pond	Brown
Hatchet Lake(Isle Royale)	Brook
Manganese Lake	Brook
No Name Pond	Brook
Siskiwit Lake(Isle Royale)	Brook

LUCE

NAME	TROUT SPECIES
Bennett Spring Pond	Brook
Brockies Pond	Brook
Buckies Pond	Brook
Bullhead Lake	Brook
Dairy Lake	Brook
Dillingham Lake	Brook
Holland Lake	Brook
Jack Lake	Brook
Little Whorl Lake	Brook
Martindary Lake	Brook
Moon Lake	Brook
Peanut Lake	Brook
Pratt Lake	Rainbow
Sid Lake	Brook
Silver Creek Pond	Brook
Spring Creek Pond	Brook
Syphon Pond	Brook
Trout Lake	Brook
Ward Lake	Brook
Wolverine Lake	Rainbow
Youngs Lake	Brook

MACKINAC

NAME	TROUT SPECIES
Castle Rock Pond	Rainbow
Millecoquins Pond	Brook
Spring Lake	Brook

MARQUETTE

NAME	TROUT SPECIES
Angeline Lake	Brook, Brown, Rainbow
Arfelin Lake	Brown, Rainbow
Bass Lake	Rainbow
Bedspring Lake	Brook
Big Trout Lake	Rainbow
Brocky Lake	Rainbow
Cecilia's Pond	Brook
Clear Lake	Brook
Cranberry Lake	Brook
Crooked Lake	Brown
Haywire Lake	Brook
Island Lake (North)	Brook
Island Lake (South)	Brook
Just Lake	Brook
Keyhole Lake (East)	Brook
Kidney Lake (South)	Brook
Lake 16	Brook
Little Brocky Lake	Rainbow
Moccasin Lake	Brook
Pauls Lake (North)	Brook
Pauls Lake (South)	Brook
Rockingchair Lake (North)	Brook
Rockingchair Lake (South)	Brook
Silver Lake	Brook
Silver Pond	Brook
Sporley Lake	Brown
Spring Lake	Brook, Rainbow

Squaw Lake	Rainbow
Strawberry Lake	Brook
Swanzy Lake	Brook
Twin Lake	Brown

ONTONAGON

NAME	TROUT SPECIES
Cooper's Pond	Brook
Courtney Lake	Brook
Johnson Lake	Brook
Lily Pond	Brook
Mirror Lake	Brook
Robbins Pond	Brown
Tanlund Lake	Rainbow
Weidman Lake	Brook

SCHOOLCRAFT

NAME	TROUT SPECIES
Banana Lake	Rainbow
Bear Lake	Rainbow
Clear Creek Pond	Brook
Dodge Lake	Rainbow
Dutch Fred Lake	Brook
Haymeadow Spring Pond	Brook
Island Lake	Rainbow
Kings Pond	Brook
Neds Lake	Brook
Twilight Lake	Brook

ADDENDUM: CONSERVATION AND PRESERVATION

As we move toward the next millennium, many of our precious natural resources are disappearing at a rapid rate. Issues pertaining to conservation and preservation of these resources have become the cornerstone for many organizations involved in protecting our environment. Lines are often drawn in the sand by political parties as each faction jockeys for position over environmental issues. As the battle rages on in congress, more and more forests and waters are ravaged each year by greed and stupidity.

Halting the assaults upon the environment takes time, unity, and capital. To fight these environmental battles on the state and national level, individuals and organizations need to unite in an effort to preserve the native inhabitants of forests and waters throughout the continental United States for future generations.

Organizations such as Trout Unlimited, the Michigan United Conservation Clubs, the National Wildlife Federation, and the Nature Conservancy have set a high standard for groups dedicated to protecting and preserving the natural resources within the beautiful state of Michigan. These groups also educate citizens on issues that are extremely critical to preserving our outdoor heritage. By joining one or more of these organizations, your voice will be heard along with the unheard whispers of the wind blowing gently through the majestic forests of Michigan.

Appendix I

Upper Peninsula DNR District Offices

District 1   (906) 353-6651
7 US 41 North
Baraga, Michigan 49908

Includes Baraga, Gogebic, Houghton, Keweenaw, and Ontonagon
counties.

District 2   (906) 875-6622
1420 US 2 West
Crystal Falls, Michigan 49920

Includes Dickinson, Iron, and Menominee counties.

District 3   (906) 786-2351
6833 Hwy. 2 41 & M-35
Gladstone, Michigan 49837

Includes Alger (West 1/2), Delta, and Marquette counties.

District 4   (906) 293-5131
Rt. 4, Box 796
Newberry, Michigan 49868

Includes Alger (East 1/2), Chippewa, Luce, Mackinac, and Schoolcraft
counties.

APPENDIX II

National Forests, Parks, and Refuges

Hiawatha National Forest   (906) 786-4062
2727 North Lincoln Road
Escanaba, MI 49829

Isle Royale National Park   (906) 482-0984
800 East Lakeshore Drive
Houghton, Michigan 49931

Ottawa Forest Headquarters   (906) 932-1330
E6248 US Highway 2
Ironwood, MI 49938

Pictured Rocks National Lakeshore   (906) 387-3700
P.O. Box 40
Munising, MI 49862-0040

Seney National Wildlife Refuge   (906) 586-9851
HCR 2 Box 1
Seney, MI 49883

APPENDIX III

USGS Map Dealers in Michigan

Ann Arbor Bivouac Inc.
336 S. State Street
Ann Arbor, MI 48104
(313) 761-6207

Ed's Sport Shop
712 N. Michigan
P.O. Box 487
Baldwin, MI 49304
(616) 745-4974

Moosejaw Mountaineering
34288 Woodward Avenue
Birmingham, MI 48009
(248) 203-7777

Boyne Country Books
125 Water Street
Boyne, MI 49712
(616) 582-3180

Keweenaw Peninsula Chamber of
Commerce
1197 Calumet Avenue
Calumet, MI 49913
(906) 337-4579

Jay's Sporting Goods
8800 S. Clare Avenue
Clare, MI 48617
(517) 386-3475

North Country Sports Inc.
103 Ontario
Detour Village, MI 49725
(906) 297-6461

Sleeping Bear Dunes NL
HWY M-72   P.O. Box 277
Empire, MI 49630
(616) 326-5134

Bay Archery Sales Co.
2713 W. Center Street
Essexville, MI 48732
(517) 894-5800

The Bookman
715 Washington Street
Grand Haven, MI 49417
(616) 846-3520

Pictured Rocks NL
Coast Guard Point Road
P.O. Box 395
Grand Marais, MI 49839
(906) 494-2669

Al and Bobs Sports Inc.
3100 S. Division Avenue
Grand Rapids, MI 49548
(616) 245-9156

Cartwright & Danewell
HWY M-72 West
P.O. Box 667
Graying, MI 49738
(517) 348-7903

Bob's Gun & Tackle Shop
2208 Gun Lake Road
Hastings, MI 49058
945-4106

Fris Office Outfitters
109 River Avenue
Holland, MI 49423
(616) 396-2341

The Outpost of Holland, Inc.
25 E. 8th Street
Holland, MI 49423
(616) 396-5556

Dicks Favorite Sports
1700 W. Memorial
Houghton, MI 49931
(906) 482-0412

Isle Royale Nat'l Park
800 E. Lakeshore Drive
Houghton, MI 49931
(906) 482-0984

Webers Sporting Goods
307 Shelden
Houghton, MI 49931
(906) 452-3121

Down Wind Sports Inc.
9010 W. Sharon Avenue
Houghton, MI 49931
(906) 482-2500

Northwoods Wilderness Outfitter
N 4088 Pine Mountain Road
Iron Mountain, MI 49801
(906) 774-9009

Blaise Erickson PE
211 Geneva Street
Ironwood, MI 49938
(906) 932-4864

Kal-Blue Reprographics
914 E. Vine Street
Kalamazoo, MI 49001
(616) 349-8681

Abrams Aerial Survey Corp.
124 N. Larch Street
P.O. Box 15008
Lansing, MI 48912
(517) 372-8100

MI Dept. of Environmental
Quality
Geological Survey Division
735 E. Hazel Street
Lansing, MI 48912
(517) 334-6943

MI United Conservation Clubs
2101 Wood Street
P.O. Box 30235
Lansing, MI 48909
(517) 371-1041

Fishermans Center
263 Arthur Street
Manistee, MI 49660
(616) 723-7718

Top O'Lake Sport Gift Shop
206 Cedar Street
Manistique, MI 49854
(906) 341-5241

Maps North
907 3rd Street
Marquette, MI 49855
(906) 226-6975

Down Wind Sports Inc.
514 N. 3rd Street
Marquette, MI 49855
(906) 482-2500

Mio Sport Shop
406 N. Morenci
Mio, MI 48647
(517) 826-3758

Wilderness Outfitter
221 W. Michigan Street
Mt Pleasant, MI 48858
(517) 773-1564

Munising Ranger District
400 E. Munising Avenue
Munising, MI 49862
(906) 387-2512

Madigan's True Value
202 Elm Avenue
Munsing, MI 49862
(906) 387-2033

G. Lengemann Co.
2314 N. 5th Street
Niles, MI 49120
(616) 684-2116

Wilderness Supply
638 River Street
Ontonagon, MI 49953
(906) 884-2922

John Rollins Books
6414 S. Westnedge Avenue
Portage, MI 49002
323-3800

Gifts and Imports Inc.
4357-A Nicolet Road
Sault Ste Marie, MI 49783
(906) 632-8745

Backcountry Outfitters
227 E. Front Street
Traverse City, MI 49684
(616) 946-1339

Delta Maps
5800 E. 12 Mile Road
Warren, MI 48092
(313) 573-8288

Eagle Response Outfitters
E21800 Wolf Lake Road
Watersmeet, MI 49969
(906) 358-4513

Sylvania Outfitters Inc.
E23423 HWY 2 West
Watersmeet, MI 49969
(906) 358-4766

Porcupine Mountain Ski Shop
1025 Superior Dr.
Box 716
White Pine, MI 49971
(906) 885-5612

SUGGESTED READINGS

Brynildson, Oscar and Robert Carline. 1977. Effects of hydraulic dredging on the ecology of native trout populations in Wisconsin Spring Ponds. Technical Bulletin No. 98, Wisconsin Department of Natural Resources, Madison.

Cordes, Ron and Randall Kaufmann. 1984. Lake Fishing With a Fly. Frank Amato Publications, Portland.

Deubler, Christopher. 1996. Trout Fishing Wisconsin Spring Ponds. Siskiwit Press, Two Rivers, Wisconsin.

Hughes, David. 1991. Strategies for Stillwater. Stackpole Books, Harrisburg.

Roberts, Donald. 1978. Nymph Fishing Lakes. Frank Amato Publications, Portland.